Happy People

Also by Brian H. Jones and published by Ginninderra Press
The Last Commando

Brian H. Jones

Happy People

From Botany Bay to Appin:
Settler perspectives on Indigenous Australians

*Happy People: From Botany Bay to Appin: Settler Perspectives on
Indigenous Australians*
ISBN 978 1 76109 081 3
Copyright © Brian Harlech-Jones 2021
Cover image by artist Elwyn Harlech-Jones, inspired by a painting by
Joseph Lycett (1774–1828)

First published 2021 by
GINNINDERRA PRESS
PO Box 3461 Port Adelaide 5015
www.ginninderrapress.com.au

Contents

Early perspectives	7
The First Fleet and the first year	19
Nature's night	50
April 1789 to 1790: wretched natives	71
The West is let in	83
Children of ignorance	108
Six heads	124
A state of war	144
Savage and inhumane	161
A look at Bennelong and Pemulwuy	177
The civilising mission	191
Conclusion	213
Works cited	218

'…happy people, content with little nay almost nothing…'
Joseph Banks, *Endeavour Journal*, 1768–1771

One
Early perspectives

In this book, I trace settlers' perspectives on Indigenous Australians during the early years of European colonisation in Australia, from 1788 until 1816. Because I have entered the busy field of publications that address aspects of the first years of colonisation in Australia, I hope to offer something that is worthwhile and different.

In researching this book, I have employed a naive approach by trying to ignore anything that I already know about the subject while relying on evidence or data that I have collected and assembled from primary sources. I do not have access to specialised databases, such as those that can be accessed via academic libraries or by working in archives, so I accessed all these sources digitally on sites that are freely available.

When I started this project, it was easy to be naive because I didn't know much about the subject. Like most amateur students of Australian colonial history, I knew something about some topics such as convicts and governors, colonial policies and events, and early explorers. However, I hadn't read or thought much about the attitudes or perspectives of early settlers.

I can't present the other side of the coin, namely the perspectives of Indigenous Australians on the settlers, because I don't have enough information. In the absence of Indigenous writing and records, any primary information would come from documents that were written by settlers and colonial officials. This means that the evidence would be limited, unreliable and partisan. Even the accounts by settlers who knew Indigenous people well, such as Buckley and Petrie, must be read with caution because they were recounted long after the events, were mediated through other pens, and were tailored to their European readers.

When I migrated to Australia during 2007, I knew very little about Indigenous Australians and equally little about relations between them and European settlers. Although I knew that settlers and Indigenous people clashed over territory, I assumed that a lot of the surface area of Australia was vacant or empty (*terra nullius*) at the time of settlement. In ignorance, I accepted this popular myth. It took me a while to realise that settlers took most of the land from the original inhabitants. Also, back in 2007, although I knew about the White Australia policy and had a general idea about discrimination against Indigenous Australians, I didn't realise how similar Australian polices were to the apartheid policies of South Africa, which was the country of my birth and my home until I was thirty-four years of age.

There was a lot that I didn't know.

Soon after I arrived in Australia, the prime minister, Kevin Rudd, led the Parliamentary Apology to the Stolen Generations– that is, the children of Australian Aboriginal and Torres Strait Islander descent who were removed from their families and communities by federal and state government agencies. This set me thinking about the complexities of the history and relationships between Indigenous and other Australians. The more I thought and read about the subject, the more complex and multifaceted it appeared to be.

A few years after we arrived in Australia, my wife Marie and I decided that we would like to satisfy our growing curiosity about Indigenous Australia by working in a remote community. During mid-2011, we got our opportunity when we worked in a small Indigenous settlement in the Kimberley region of Western Australia. It was in a remote location, nearly 200 kilometres by dirt road from the nearest town, and about 500 kilometres from the nearest sizeable town with facilities such as banks and dentists.

Here, we met many people who were living challenged lives in challenging conditions. In many respects, our experience resonated with, for instance, the report 'Overcoming Indigenous Disadvantage' (2016), which was produced by the Australian Government Productivity Commission. This report compared data from 2014 to 2016 and concluded that

> The proportion of adults reporting high levels of psychological distress increased from 27 per cent in 2004–05 to 33 per cent in 2014–15, and hospitalisations for self-harm increased by 56 per cent over this period.

These findings agree with Maggie White's conclusions in her 2011 report on conditions in the Fitzroy Valley, in Western Australia's Kimberley region. She wrote,

> In traumatised populations such as those that have experienced war, dispossession and other catastrophic events the whole spectrum of attachment styles gets shifted towards the insecure. Instead of a majority with secure attachment styles, there develops a majority who do not see the world as a fundamentally good place. The levels of suicidal despair and other mental distress in the Fitzroy Valley would point to that shift as having already taken place.

Our settlement was about 300 kilometres from the Fitzroy Valley, with which it shared many cultural and historical ties.

Although our experience was stressful, it was also thought-provoking. Before long, I wanted to understand why things are the way they are. And slowly, as I reflected, and as I read and thought and talked to people, I developed the idea for this book.

I came to understand that the quality of Indigenous life began to deteriorate from the moment that Europeans first settled the continent during January 1788. As a result, even today, many Indigenous people, who are members of a cultural group that operated in self-sufficient autonomy for scores of thousands of years, seem to fit Maggie White's description of people who 'do not see the world as a fundamentally good place'. Why did it happen? How did it happen? Why were the consequences of settlement so severe?

When we try to understand a complex situation, it is often useful to begin at the beginning. That is why I went back to the first years of colonisation. I adopted a naive approach, mainly using primary sources, because I wanted to try to form my own view about what happened, and why.

I said that the quality of Indigenous life began to deteriorate from the moment that Europeans first settled the continent. If so, what were things like before that? To get a picture, we must rely on written sources by outsiders, most of them European. One of the most comprehensive accounts is in Joseph Banks's *Endeavour* journal. It is also a good place to start, because Banks was a prime mover in the initiative to establish the original penal colony in what came to be called Australia.

During 1770, the crew and scientists of James Cook's *Endeavour* spent seven weeks at the site of today's Cooktown in northern Queensland where they stopped to repair the ship after a close encounter with a coral reef. Banks got to know some of the members of the local Guugu Yimithirr group and wrote this about them:

> Thus live these I had almost said happy people, content with little nay almost nothing, Far enough removd from the anxieties attending upon riches, or even the possession of what we Europeans call common necessaries...

Banks saw no evidence of alienation, dissonance and dependency. On the contrary, he portrayed the Indigenous people that he encountered as independent, grounded, self-sufficient, and at ease with themselves and their environment. Also, they valued and protected their country and its resources.

How things changed, and how quickly! In 1845, seventy-five years after Banks wrote those words, and only fifty-seven years after European settlement began, John Eyre expressed regret at the condition of Indigenous people. He wrote that they had once evinced 'the fearless courage and proud demeanor which a life of independence and freedom always inspires' but no longer. Eyre continued by describing the sad condition of Indigenous people under settler domination in these poignant words:

> They are strangers in their own land and possess no longer the usual

means of procuring their daily subsistence; hungry, and famished, they wander about begging…

In less than sixty years, the state of Indigenous people who were in contact with Europeans deteriorated to the point where they were 'strangers in their own land'. As European intrusion continued to expand across the continent, so more and more Indigenous people were affected until finally, with the occupation of remote regions such as the Kimberley and the Gulf Country during the 1880s, almost no Indigenous group had escaped.

The first recorded contact between Indigenous people and Europeans on the east coast of mainland Australia took place on 29 April 1770, at Botany Bay near Sydney (as the places are now called) when Cook and some of his men landed to contact a group of Indigenous people on the shore. Although most of the natives left the scene – Cook wrote that 'they all made off' – two men remained to oppose the landing. Cook wrote,

> as soon as we put the boat in they again came to oppose us, upon which I fir'd a musquet between the 2, which had no other Effect than to make them retire back, where bundles of their darts lay, and one of them took up a stone and threw at us, which caused my firing a Second Musquet, load with small Shott; and altho' some of the shott struck the man, yet it had no other effect than making him lay hold on a Target [shield].

On the following day, one of the ship's officers tried to contact the 'natives' by offering them gifts; however, wrote Cook, 'it was to no purpose…'

This was the pattern for the rest of the Europeans' stay in Botany Bay. The Indigenous people either retreated into cover as the strangers approached or, in the case of some of the men, shadowed the newcomers while avoiding contact. When Cook sailed from Botany Bay, he wrote,

> we could know but very little of their Customs, as we never were

able to form any Connections with them; they had not so much as touch'd the things we had left in their Hutts on purpose for them to take away.

The encounter was not encouraging. It began with aggression, after which the Indigenous people kept their distance from the Europeans. Also, far from appreciating the gifts that the Europeans left for them, such as 'Cloth, Looking Glasses, Coombs, Beads, Nails, etc.', the local people simply left them untouched. Cook summed up the encounter in these words: '…all they seem'd to want was for us to be gone'. In the future, this assessment would be repeated many times.

Later, during June 1770, while tentatively navigating through the shoals and reefs of the Great Barrier Reef, HMS *Endeavour* ran aground on coral. Everyone on board felt that they were doomed. Even if they managed to make it to dry land, they did not know what awaited them there. Banks recorded that he was fearful that, deprived of arms and ammunition, they would be annihilated by the local people, whom he termed 'the most uncivilizd savages perhaps in the world'.

After a nerve-racking struggle, they managed to float off the reef and worked the damaged ship toward a nearby river mouth. While waiting for a fair wind to take them into the river, Banks felt more hopeful; he wrote,

> At night we observd a fire ashore near where we were to lay, which made us hope that the necessary length of our stay would give us an oportunity of being acquainted with the Indians who made it.

The 'Indians' were in no hurry to become acquainted with these uninvited visitors. It was twenty-two days before the first encounter took place, about which Banks wrote,

> Four Indians appeard on the opposite shore; they had with them a Canoe made of wood with an outrigger in which two of them embarkd and came towards the ship…

The men approached slowly and cautiously until they were alongside. The Europeans gave them gifts of 'Cloth, Nails, Paper, etc.' and Banks recorded that when they took the gifts, they did not show 'the least signs of satisfaction'. They only expressed emotion when they were given a small fish; then, wrote Banks,

> they expressd the greatest joy imaginable, and instantly putting off from the ship made signs that they would bring over their comrades...

It is not clear why, after staying aloof for twenty-two days, the local people finally decided to approach the newcomers. Perhaps, after observing the situation, they were reasonably confident that the newcomers did not intend to infringe further on land and resources. Perhaps, also, it was because they wanted to discover the habits and intentions of the newcomers. Perhaps curiosity finally got the better of them.

Daily encounters followed, with increasing familiarity on both sides, although the Europeans were never allowed to approach women and children. Eight days after the first meeting, Banks wrote,

> Indians were over with us today and seemd to have lost all fear of us and became quite familiar...they venturd on board the ship and soon became our very good friends...

However, the good relations were disturbed next day, when ten men came on board and demanded one of the turtles that the sailors had caught. Banks wrote that the visitors displayed 'great marks of Resentment' while one man 'pushd me from him with a countenance full of disdain'. When they were unable to get a turtle, after a show of great annoyance – Cook wrote that 'they grew a little Troublesome, and were for throwing every thing overboard they could lay their hands upon' – the men disembarked and, in rage, set fire to the grass around the Europeans' camp on shore. To drive the men away, Cook fired a musket and struck one man with small shot, after which he shot a musket ball into the undergrowth as a warning.

Turtles are large, nutritious animals that were hunted and appreciated by the Indigenous people, as Cook and his shipmates well knew.

The local men showed resentment and hostility when they were refused a turtle because this was their country and they had sole right to all the produce of the land and sea in their domain. Outsiders could only access these resources if they were granted permission. However, the Europeans had not only taken up residence unannounced but had also wantonly helped themselves to other people's resources.

Following the dispute over the turtle, an old man approached, carrying a blunt lance. Banks described the encounter as follows:

> He halted several times and as he stood employd himself in collecting the moisture from under his arm pit with his finger which he every time drew through his mouth. We beckond to him to come: he then spoke to the others who all laid their lances against a tree and leaving them came forwards likewise and soon came quite to us.

It was a remarkable moment in which the old man acted as a peacemaker. Although some of the men from the earlier encounter disappeared, three newcomers joined the group. Banks continued,

> The Strangers were presented to us by name and we gave them such trinkets as we had about us; then we all proceeded towards the ship, they making signs as they came along that they would not set fire to the grass again and we distributing musquet balls among them and by our signs explaining their effect.

The Indigenous men would not board the ship and departed about two hours later.

The Guugu Yimithirr people gave the Europeans at least four clear messages. One: if you try to occupy our country, we will resist you. Two: you may only use our resources with our permission. Three: we want nothing from you. Four: most of all, we want you to be gone. Did the Europeans get the message? Largely, they had the experience but missed the meaning (to quote T.S. Eliot) because they were operating within a different paradigm and with different assumptions.

After the ship had been repaired, while sailing around the northern extremity of Australia, Cook went ashore on an island in the Torres Straits and annexed the whole east coast down to 38 degrees latitude 'in the name of His Majesty'. (Thirty-eight degrees latitude crosses the country between modern-day Canberra and the border of the state of Victoria.) In his journal, Cook wrote that he was confident that the east coast

> was never seen or Visited by any European before us; and notwithstanding I had in the Name of his Majesty taken possession of several places upon this Coast, I now once More hoisted English Colours, and in the Name of His Majesty King George the Third took possession of the whole Eastern coast from the above Latitude down to this place by the Name of New Wales...

Later, in the royal commission of 12 October 1786 by which Arthur Phillip was appointed as governor of the new colony of New South Wales, the territory was redefined to cover an even larger area.

Cook's and Banks's journals introduced several themes that were ominous harbingers of fraught future relationships between Indigenous people and Europeans. Firstly, Cook annexed the country without any consideration of the fact that it was already inhabited. His only concern was whether another European country had staked a claim. In other words, Europeans were entitled to occupy, rule and exploit the resources of any region of the world that was not already occupied or claimed by Europeans. Only Europeans had sovereign rights; non-Europeans did not have rights to territory, security or self-governance.

Secondly, Europeans regarded Indigenous Australians as savages; as seen above, Banks called them 'the most uncivilizd savages perhaps in the world'. The term 'savage', which Europeans commonly applied to indigenous people, was used again, as it often was, when the commander of the First Fleet, Arthur Phillip, was instructed that when he arrived in Botany Bay, he should 'open an intercourse with the Savages'.

The designation 'savage' is central to understanding the mindset of Europeans in relation to colonialism and expansionism. A key concept was the hierarchy of civilisation, with Europeans at the top and savages at the bottom. We see this, for instance, in Darwin's comment in *Voyage of the Beagle* (1839) that Indigenous people in Australia appeared to be a few degrees higher in 'the scale of civilisation' than the Fuegians, of whom Darwin wrote,

> I would not have believed how entire the difference between savage and civilized man is... It is greater than between a wild and domesticated animal, in as much as in man there is greater power of improvement.

In Darwin's view, the Fuegians ranked lower on the ladder of civilisation than the Australian Indigenous people, while both ranked a long way below civilised people. Darwin's reference to improvement is also significant because it denoted a widely held view that European individuals and societies were not only capable of improvement and progress but were also capable of improving the new lands and peoples that they occupied, whereas savages were incapable on all counts. Savages could not improve through their own efforts and resources and were static on the bottom rungs of the ladder of civilisation. However, they could improve if superior civilisations intervened to show the way.

Although Europeans opined that all non-Europeans were less civilised than they were, there was disagreement about ranking on the ladder. For instance, while a First Fleeter, David Blackburn, labelled the Indigenous people of NSW as 'to All Appearance the Lowest in Rank Among the Human Race', Watkins Tench, who sailed as a marine officer with the First Fleet, named the indigenous African people of the eastern coastal regions of South Africa (Europeans called them Caffres or Kaffers) as 'the most savage set of brutes on earth'. However, later he ranked Indigenous Australians below Africans. Whatever the case, Europeans believed they were at the top of the hierarchy and savages occupied the lowest rungs.

This preoccupation with rankings and grades of civilisation was found wherever Europeans were on colonising missions. Hamburg-born Hinrich Lichtenstein, who travelled in South Africa during the first decade of the nineteenth century, wrote,

There is not perhaps any class of savages upon the earth that lead lives so near those of the brutes as the *Bosjesmans* [Bushmen]; none perhaps who are sunk so low, who are so unimportant in the scale of existence; whose wants, whose cares, and whose joys, are so low in their nature; and who are consequently so little capable of cultivation.

To this, he added that Bushmen more resembled apes than humans. Lichtenstein also wrote that during their travels near the Orange River, which was then beyond the borders of the Cape Colony, he and his companions visited a settlement that was occupied by Bastards, who were people of mixed indigenous and Dutch ancestry, and Bushmen. He commented that the former lived in lived in 'large clean huts, and were clothed in linen or woollen cloth' while the latter lived in 'dirty *pandoks* and had skins thrown over them'. (*Pandok* was a derogatory term for a flimsy, insubstantial hut.) Lichtenstein meant that people with a proportion of European ancestry, namely the Bastards, were superior to those without any.

Moodie, an Englishman who visited South Africa during the 1830s, expressed a similar opinion about a hierarchy of cultures when he described the indigenous Khoi people (also called by the derogatory name Hottentots) as providing a 'deplorable and degrading picture of human nature' and occupying a position 'beneath the more favoured race' – that is, Europeans. Almost a century after Lichtenstein, an Englishman, Massie, wrote in the same vein that the Bushmen were 'pigmies in stature, and very low down in the scale of civilisation'. Above them, he placed the Hottentots, who were 'vastly superior in every way to the Bushmen'.

Believing that they occupied the highest rung on the scale of civilisation, Europeans considered that they had both a right and a mission to civilise races and peoples who were not similarly advantaged. By civilise, Europeans meant elevating the savages to the point where they lived, thought, dressed, worshipped and spoke like their European mentors – in fact, to the point where the savages were cultural clones of Europeans. However, even at that point, the newly elevated savages were not accorded full rights and recognition because, as new arrivals to the condition, they were regarded as unstable and unreliable. They were still too close to their earlier condition, which flawed their new condition and to which they could too easily revert.

Tuckey, who was a member of the party that attempted to establish a penal colony at Port Phillip during 1803, encompassed the themes of entitlement, superiority in the hierarchy, and improvement when, while at Port Phillip, he wrote,

> when I contrasted the powers, the ingenuity, and the resources of civilized man, with the weakness, the ignorance, and the wants of the savage he came to dispossess, I acknowledged the immensity of human intelligence, and felt thankful for the small portion dispensed to myself.

Here, Tuckey artlessly admitted that the colonists came to dispossess the Indigenous people. Imagining the improvements that would follow when the settlement was established, he fantasised about

> a second Rome, rising from a coalition of *banditti* [convicts]. I beheld it giving laws to the world, and superlative in arms and in arts…

A further, ominous harbinger of fraught relations is seen in Banks's observation that Indigenous people were 'content with little nay almost nothing' and made do without 'what we Europeans call common necessaries.'. This assessment, which was quite common among Europeans who commented on Indigenous life and culture, might seem to be a complimentary and sympathetic comment on the self-sufficiency and self-sustaining nature of Indigenous society. It might even be regarded as expressing admiration for the noble savage. However, the contrary is true, because it provided the rationale for regarding Indigenous people as uncivilised and undeveloped. It showed that they, and the land on which they lived, and which sustained them, were undeveloped and therefore were ripe to be developed and improved so that they, too, would desire the common necessaries that came with being civilised.

Two

The First Fleet and the first year

When convicts could no longer be transported to America after the American Revolution, the British government selected Botany Bay for its new penal colony. This began European settlement in Australia.

During January 1788, the eleven ships of the First Fleet sailed into Botany Bay. Of the approximately 1,400 people on board, about half were convicts, while the remainder were officers, crew members, soldiers and family members.

Captain Arthur Phillip, commander of the fleet and governor of the colony, was instructed to 'open an intercourse with the Savages' and to ensure that the colonists lived 'in amity and kindness' with them. However, the goodwill of the native people was not taken for granted: one of the duties of the Marine contingent that accompanied the Fleet was 'the defence of the settlement against the incursion of the natives'. Later, a representation dated 21 December 1786 (that is, while preparations were under way) to the home secretary, Lord Sydney, suggested that the military force should be enlarged, partly because of

> the uncertain dispositions of the natives, who may be naturally presumed hostile to strangers forming a settlement among them, and are certainly formidable and numerous, from the immense tract of country they possess.

In addition, on 28 February 1787, Phillip noted to Lord Sydney,

> On landing in Botany Bay it will be necessary to throw up a slight work as a defence against the natives – who, tho' only seen in small numbers by Captain Cook, may be very numerous on other parts of the coast.

In summary, although the colonisers would display amity and kindness, it was assumed that the natives would be hostile and would resist colonisation.

Further, Phillip was instructed that portions of the corn and seed grain in the ships should be used for cultivation, that the domestic animals on board should be used for breeding purposes, and that cultivation should begin immediately after arrival. Specifically, he was instructed to

> proceed to the cultivation of the land, distributing the convicts for that purpose in such manner…as may appear to you to be necessary and best calculated for procuring supplies of grain and ground provisions.

Also, land should be surveyed to provide allotments for emancipated convicts, viz.

> To every Male shall be granted, 30 Acres of land, and in case he shall be married, 20 Acres more, and for every child who may be with them at the Settlement, at the time of making the said Grant, a further quantity of 10 Acres…

If we accept Phillip's estimate that there were about 1,500 Indigenous people in the Harbour region, then the people who disembarked from the ships nearly doubled the population of the region, literally overnight. It is almost impossible to imagine the incredulity, horror and outrage with which the traditional owners of the land would have regarded this sudden imposition. Nor can we imagine the strain that an instantaneous doubling of the population placed on resources and living space.

Among the many violations that were perpetrated by this sudden invasion was the fact that Indigenous sacred sites were spread all over Indigenous country. These sites were inextricably linked to Indigenous beliefs about origins and human existence, and were cared for by elders, who were repositories of wisdom and law. Indigenous people would been outraged at the fact that the newcomers were violating and desecrating many of these sites.

The instructions to Phillip provided the tinder for the fire that would burn its destructive path through Indigenous life for the time to come. The colony would begin by appropriating enough land and resources to house and feed more than 1,400 people. Next, it would expand indefinitely as ever more resources were needed, such as timber, stone, clay, other building materials, firewood, fish, bush vegetables, and wild meat, and as ever more land would be allocated to emancipated convicts, soldiers who had completed their service, and free settlers. It was delusory to think that it would be possible to live in 'amity and kindness' with people whose land and resources were being occupied and exploited, whose country was being violated, and who were being evicted. How could the victims live peacefully and contentedly with the thieves?

Tench described the scene on the first day of settlement in Sydney Cove as follows:

> Business now sat on every brow, and the scene, to an indifferent spectator, at leisure to contemplate it, would have been highly picturesque and amusing. In one place, a party cutting down the woods; a second, setting up a blacksmith's forge; a third, dragging along a load of stones or provisions; here an officer pitching his marquee, with a detachment of troops parading on one side of him, and a cook's fire blazing up on the other.

Tench continued by describing how the convicts constructed numerous little edifices. This was only a beginning, as Tench enthused about grand plans:

> To proceed on a narrow, confined scale, in a country of the extensive limits we possess, would be unpardonable: extent of empire demands grandeur of design…the principal street in our projected city will be, when completed, agreeable to the plan laid down, two hundred feet in breadth, and all the rest of a corresponding proportion.

Tench's statement, 'in a country of the extensive limits we possess… extent of empire demands grandeur of design' expressed pride of untrammelled ownership, even though the authorities in Britain, and the settlers, knew that the land was already inhabited.

Whatever the traditional owners of the land thought about the events, they would not have considered them to be 'picturesque and amusing'. Instead, they would have been surprised, offended and angry when, without even a by your leave, the colonists began to establish a permanent settlement in country that was not theirs.

To understand the enormity of the dislocation that was wrought by Europeans, it is useful to recall the relationship between Indigenous groups and country. Tom Petrie, who was well acquainted with Indigenous customs and beliefs during the early days of European settlement in the Brisbane region – as a boy, he learned the local language and fraternised extensively with Indigenous people – described the situation like this:

> Each tribe had its own boundary, which was well known, and none went to hunt, etc., on another's property without an invitation, unless they knew they would be welcome, and sent special messengers to announce their arrival… The tribe in general owned the animals and birds on the ground, also roots and nests, but certain men and women owned different fruit or flower-trees and shrubs.

European occupation rode roughshod over all this: it was the equivalent of a home invasion, where the intruders took up permanent residence, making free with the resources, including prized possessions, and putting up their own structures on site. All this was done in the face of the owners who, being weaker and fewer in number, either accepted the intrusion (which was unlikely), or resisted, or departed. If they resisted, they were subjected by superior force, usually with loss of life.

A contributing factor to the dislocation was that Indigenous clans or groups were often numerically small and usually occupied relatively small territories, particularly in more fertile areas such as those near the coast.

As seen above, each emancipated convict, married with one child, was to be given sixty acres. Also, allocations would be made to free settlers (beginning during 1793) while further allocations would be made to military personnel who completed their contracts and chose to remain in NSW. Before long, much larger grants were made to officers and favoured free settlers. Each allocation would squeeze Indigenous people into an even smaller space and would disrupt their movements and patterns of resource-gathering. For instance, a few adjoining allocations could almost completely sever one part of traditional land from another part. Also, the allocations would embrace only the best and most fertile parts of a clan's territory, and there would be supplementary encroachments, for purposes such as roads and paths, tree-felling and collecting wood, commercial and official purposes (for example, establishing shops, inns, schools, courthouses), and hunting, among others. The original inhabitants would either become serfs on their own land or would become fugitives who would press on neighbouring groups, with knock-on effects, causing both cultural and spatial dislocations. Unlike some conquests that leave the inhabitants in place and allow day-to-day lives to go on relatively intact, this one, which was a full-scale occupation with ever-increasing numbers of settlers, appropriated all the resources and left almost no living space for the original inhabitants.

Early during the third year of settlement, 1790, more extensive offers of land were made to encourage enlisted men who completed their terms of service to remain in the colony.

> To every non-commissioned officer, an allotment of one hundred and thirty acres of land if single, and one hundred and fifty if married.
>
> To every private man, eighty acres of land if single, one hundred if married; and ten acres of land for each child at the time of granting the allotment.
>
> To any man who enlisted in the new corps, 'an allotment of double the above proportion of land if they behaved well for five year'. (Collins)

The demand for land and resources was insatiable.

The dislocation was exacerbated when the settlement at Rose Hill (Parramatta), about thirty kilometres from Sydney Cove, was founded during the first year. Transportation routes and associated developments from Sydney Cove to Rose Hill led right through Indigenous land, traversing the territory that belonged to the Wangal clan, if Phillip's classification of tribes was correct (see later). In addition, seine netting by the settlers was depleting the fish stocks in the Harbour. For instance, during the first winter in the settlement, Hunter wrote,

> ...the want of a little fresh food for the Sick is very much felt, and fish at this time are very Scarse, such of the Natives as we meet seem to be in a Miserable and Starving Condition from that Scarsity...

Further, at the beginning of the third winter (April 1790) Tench recorded that food supplies in the settlement had run so low that all the boats were employed in fishing, and that 'all the officers, civil and military, including the clergyman, and the surgeons of the hospital' offered to go out in the boats every night to catch as much fish as possible. In addition, 'The best marksmen of the marines and convicts were also selected, ...with directions to range the woods in search of kangaroos.' This was happening at the same time as the smallpox was causing devastation among Indigenous people. Clearly, the colony made it ever more difficult for the original inhabitants of the Harbour area to maintain traditional ways, or even just survive.

When Phillip left the settlement during October 1792, the population of the mainland settlement (that is, excluding Norfolk Island) had increased to more than 3,000. Branch settlements had been established at Parramatta and Toongabbie, and 1,500 acres of land had been brought under cultivation.

To return to the beginning, after arriving at Botany Bay, Phillip went ashore and met a group of Indigenous people. In his journal, he wrote,

They were all armed, but on seeing the Governor approach [Phillip wrote in the third person] with signs of friendship, alone and unarmed, they readily returned his confidence by laying down their weapons... The presents offered by their new visitors were all readily accepted, nor did any kind of disagreement arise while the ships remained in Botany Bay.

Buoyed by the encounter, Phillip expressed the hope that

a sanguinary temper was no longer to disgrace the European settlers in countries newly discovered.

This time it was going to be different. Conflicts and hostilities would be avoided, and amity and kindness would prevail. It was wishful thinking.

There were other, different accounts of the first contacts. From his ship, Bradley saw that while Phillip was ashore, the sailors mingled with native people on the beach in a friendly fashion and

amused themselves with dressing the natives with paper and other whimsical things to entertain them, with which they were well pleased for the moment.

However, next day the mood changed when a boat party went ashore for water. Bradley reported,

The natives were well pleased with our People until they began clearing the Ground, at which they were displeased and wanted them to be gone.

Similarly, in his journal, White reported an incident in Botany Bay when sailors hauled a net up the beach after trawling in the bay. When the natives saw the catch, they gave a shout 'expressive of astonishment and joy'. However, this was followed by discord:

No sooner were the fish out of the water than they [the natives] began to lay hold of them, as if they had a right to them, or that they were their own...

'As if they had a right to them…': there, in a nutshell, was the source of the conflict that would soon erupt. Both parties needed the land and sea to survive, and both parties believed that they had the right to these resources. To the Indigenous people, the settlers were uninvited interlopers on land that they had called home since time immemorial; to the British, the Indigenous people were savages who came with the territory that had been annexed for the Crown. In the view of the colonists, the savages had no more claim on the land and resources than did cockatoos, kangaroos and wombats.

The fishing net incident replicated the quarrel over the turtles that Banks recorded eighteen years earlier at Endeavour River. Bradley's and White's observations suggested that although the Indigenous inhabitants were wary at first, they were not actively hostile. However, their attitude changed when the newcomers began to clear the ground and to catch fish because, as had been the case with the turtles on the *Endeavour*, these were intrusions on resources that Indigenous people claimed as their own. However, the Europeans did not understand the reactions because they recognised no claims or rights but their own.

How can we interpret the fact that the native men on the beach allowed the sailors to decorate them with 'paper and other whimsical things'? It could be that the sailors were treating the Indigenous people like children or pets – or perhaps as men in a male-dominated culture would treat the weaker sex. This view can be corroborated by later incidents, in which sailors amused themselves by playing practical jokes on Indigenous men. It could also be that lacking a common language, each party was trying to make sense of the other by various means. On the other hand, the Indigenous people might have thought that the paper and other whimsical things were part of a greeting ceremony. We can only speculate, because there is no record of Indigenous reactions to these encounters. Nor is there a record of the sailors' motives.

After observing the activities on shore in Botany Bay, Worgan expressed the opinion that the native people were simple and childlike when he wrote that the Indigenous men received the objects

...with much the same kind of Pleasure, which Children shew at such Bawbles, just looking at them, then holding out their Hands for more, some laughing heartily, and jumping extravagantly...

Then, commenting on the incident in which sailors decorated native men with 'different coloured Papers, and Fools Caps', Worgan stated that

the strange contrast these Decorations made with their black Complexion brought strongly to my Mind, the Chimney-Sweepers in London on a May-Day.

While these interactions demonstrated the depth of the misunderstandings – perhaps misconstructions – between the two parties, the clearest portent of future conflict was the way in which the Europeans not only came ashore without asking permission, but also freely appropriated the natural resources by clearing the ground and fishing in the bay. To put it into perspective, they would never have done this on the coasts of, say, France or Germany. Landing on those coasts without permission would have been treated as a hostile action and resisted with force – just as it was in New South Wales.

At that time, two French ships arrived in Botany Bay. From the commander, Phillip heard that twelve of the Frenchmen had been killed in a skirmish in Samoa. He reflected on the encounter as follows:

This fatal result from too implicit a confidence, may, perhaps very properly, increase the caution of Europeans in their commerce with savages, but ought not to excite suspicion. The resentments of such people are sudden and sanguinary, and, where the intercourse of language is wanting, may easily be awakened by misapprehension: but it seems possible to treat them with sufficient marks of confidence, without abandoning the guards of prudence.

It was forward of Phillip to opine with such certainty about the characteristics of people about whom he, and everyone in his party, had little knowledge. It looks as if he was drawing on a common stereotype of savages, namely that they were emotionally volatile and quick to anger but easy to placate if handled properly. Also, they recognised superior authority.

Soon after, while exploring the harbour to find a site for a permanent base, Phillip again interacted with a group of native people and reported,

> These also were armed with lances, and at first were very vociferous; but the same gentle means used towards the others easily persuaded these also to discard their suspicions, and to accept whatsoever was offered.

On shore, when the Indigenous people crowded around the newcomers too closely, no doubt out of curiosity, Phillip drew a circle on the ground to mark the boundary between the two parties and reported that 'they sat down in perfect quietness'. This, wrote Phillip, was

> Another proof how tractable these people are, when no insult or injury is offered, and when proper means are [sic] to influence the simplicity of their minds.

Amity and kindness prevailed – in Phillip's mind, anyway. With their simple minds, it was easy to influence and manage the natives.

At first, the Indigenous people around the harbour were not hostile toward the newcomers. Writing of events less than a week after the settlers went ashore in Port Jackson, Bowes noted that while Captain Hunter and a boat party were exploring the shoreline of the harbour, they met about 100 native men and women, 'who presented the Captain and Gentlemen that were with him, with Laurel leaves and behaved very friendly'. In return, the Europeans put beads around the women's necks and 'gave them other trinckets'.

Of the settlement itself, Tench noted, 'The Indians for a little while after our arrival paid us frequent visits.' However, other observers recorded only one visit. Bradley noted that two weeks after settlement began, on 8 February, 'Two Natives came to the Camp, the Governor gave a Hatchet and several other things but could not persuade them to stay.' Also, Bowes reported that on 9 February (but it reads like the same visit as reported by Bradley), two Indigenous men, who were 'pretty much advanced in life' and carried spears, sat down near the camp but would not enter it. The governor and some officers went to them, presented one of them with a hatchet, and 'bound some red Bunting about their heads with some yellow Tinfoil'. Simple savages loved cheap, brightly coloured adornments that would divert their attention while the donors were stealing their country! Bowes continued that although the men were sitting near the governor's house, they did not show any interest in it. Also, they appeared to be at their ease – perhaps studiously at ease – as shown by the fact that one of them took time to sharpen the point of his spear with an oyster shell. This action, which might have had significance in Aboriginal culture, with its air of quiet menace and assurance, suggested that the men were showing that they belonged in this locality.

While the men were there, 'a black Boy…came up to look at them'. The men felt his hair, opened his shirt to examine his chest, and indicated that they wanted a lock of his hair. Bowes complied, and then cut off some of the men's hair. After that, wrote Bowes, 'They stay'd here at least an hour then betook themselves into the woods, and nobody has been near the Camp since.' This observation was corroborated by Tench, who wrote that within a few days 'they [Indigenous people] were observed to be more shy of our company'.

The visit was a reconnaissance, to find out what the visitors were doing and what were their intentions. When it became clear that the Europeans intended to stay, the Indigenous people detached themselves and refused to have anything more to do with the newcomers. This is suggested by Bowes's report that at about the same date as the above encounter, Indigenous people showed hostility for the first time when they opposed a boat party that was fishing in a cove 'near the Entrance of the Harbour' by pelting them with stones and threatening them with spears. It is reasonable to infer that the Indigenous clan that lived around Sydney Cove had decided that it was unable to oppose the large number of people who had settled there, and so could only reconnoitre and then ring-fence the settlement. Tench wrote, almost certainly correctly, that the fact that the Indigenous people did not attack the settlement could only be explained by 'their knowledge of our numbers, and their dread of our fire-arms'. However, news having spread quickly, Indigenous people in other areas of the Harbour were forewarned and were determined to resist attempts at settlement in their lands. For instance, soon after arrival, Hunter reported more hostility while he and a boat party were exploring the upper reaches of the Harbour, when

> vast Numbers of Arm'd Men appeard upon the Shore wherever we approached it, and in a threatening Manner, seemed to insist upon our not presuming to land...

Despite some friendly contacts, the generally hostile attitude continued throughout the first year and longer. For instance, in a dispatch to Lord Sydney dated 28 September 1788, Phillip stated that

> as I have ever found them, since they find we intend to remain, they appeared best pleased when we were leaving them, though I gave them many useful articles; and it is not possible to say whether it was from fear or contempt that they do not come amongst us.

Phillip understood that the Indigenous people's hostility emanated from their understanding that the Europeans were there to stay and, as he put it eloquently, were 'Best pleased when we were leaving them...' More than anyone, Phillip sometimes saw right through to the heart of a matter, even if he invariably backtracked when he readjusted his compass to align with his mission and instructions.

Indigenous hostility was not confined to the Harbour region. Bradley wrote that on 21 February 1788, about one month after the French ships under Lapérouse arrived in Botany Bay, some French officers visited Governor Phillip and told him that 'the Natives are exceedingly troublesome there and that wherever they meet an unarmed Man they attack him'. Clearly, the French expedition had overstayed and had exceeded the tolerance level of the people around Botany Bay, who were in close contact with the Harbour people. It was time for the visitors to be gone.

A similar pattern of behaviour was noted by Tuckey when there was an abortive attempt to establish a penal colony at Port Phillip during 1803. When the colonists arrived, the Indigenous people were friendly and curious; Tuckey wrote that some Indigenous people

> came to the boats entirely unarmed, and without the smallest symptom of apprehension; presents of blankets biscuits etc. were given to them, with which, except in one instance, they departed satisfied and inoffensive.

However, not long afterward, when boat parties were exploring the shores of the bay,

> upwards of two hundred natives assembled round the surveying boats, and their obviously hostile intentions made the application of fire-arms absolutely necessary to repel them, by which one native was killed, and two or three wounded.

Tuckey also described other determined and fierce actions to prevent the Europeans from remaining on shore.

Testifying to just how quickly Indigenous attitudes toward the settlers changed, Bowes wrote that on 28 February at 'a Cove a great distance from Sydney Cove', a fishing party in a boat was received in friendly fashion by Indigenous people, who helped to draw the seine net and made a fire to cook some of the fish. However, only a few days later, on 4 March, he noted that 'the Natives were very troublesome to our Sailors hauling the Seyne at a Cove near the mouth of the Harbour'. Also, Bowes wrote that on the same day he learned that 'the Natives had kill'd several of the Convicts who had elop'd from Port Jackson and taken up their residence near Botany Bay'. Five days later, wrote Bowes, a sailor who was lost in the bush was stripped and treated so roughly by Indigenous people that he only just escaped with his life.

From the first days of the settlement, there was a difference between the attitudes towards the Indigenous people of authority figures (Tench terms them people in higher stations) on the one hand, and those who were in subordinate positions on the other hand. This was already apparent in the different accounts of the activities on the shore of Botany Bay. Bradley, who was a first lieutenant, and White and Worgan, who were surgeons, were less restrained in their observations than Phillip.

In trying to implement the instructions that governed the expedition, authority figures struggled to preserve the illusion that it was possible to invade and occupy the country while also establishing and maintaining friendly relations with the colonised people. They, Phillip especially, were suffering from cognitive dissonance, which is the mental stress or discomfort experienced by an individual who holds two or more contradictory beliefs, ideas or values at the same time. A major reason for their dissonance was that their professional reputations and positions depended on their being able to report to their superiors in London that things were going according to plan. If London wanted a policy of amity and kindness, then actions and events that did not fit the pattern would be treated as aberrations and not as the norm. Another reason was that all human beings try to justify their repressive and distasteful actions by cloaking them with more acceptable-sounding motives, or by explaining them in terms of necessity, exigency, external pressure, and so on.

On 28 February 1787, before the Fleet sailed, Phillip set out his agenda for relations with the Indigenous people when he wrote to Lord Sydney,

> I shall think it a great point gained if I can proceed in this business without having any dispute with the natives, a few of which I shall endeavour to pursuade to settle near us, and who I mean to furnish with everything that can tend to civilize them, and to give them a high opinion of the new guests…

Was the use of the word 'guests' ironic? Apparently not.

Throughout his tenure as governor, although Phillip recognised that the Indigenous people were resisting colonisation, he would hardly ever admit it. His formal position remained as he expressed it two weeks after settlement, on 7 February 1788, when he wrote that he was determined, if possible, to bring even the native inhabitants of New South Wales into a voluntary subjection; or at least to establish with them a strict amity and alliance.

Further, he wrote that

induced by motives of humanity, it was his determination from his first landing, to treat them with the utmost kindness: and he was firmly resolved, that, whatever differences might arise, nothing less than the most absolute necessity should ever compel him to fire upon them.

On 9 March 1788, six weeks after arriving in Port Jackson, Phillip still maintained that his project of amity and kindness was on track. After a tour of the coastal regions of the Harbour, he wrote that he had 'maintained an intercourse with the natives without departing from his favourite plan of treating them with the utmost kindness'. However, he expressed misgivings when he wrote that 'he could have no reason to reproach himself' if his efforts were negated 'by the wanton profligacy of some depraved individuals'. In plain language, it would not be his fault if his well-intentioned efforts were undone by the provocative actions of others. He was thinking of the convicts who, he was convinced, treated the Indigenous people in a rough and cavalier fashion.

Of course, the convicts were sent into the bush unarmed, where they were exposed to the anger of the Indigenous people.

Soon afterwards, two convicts who had gone into the bush searching for vegetables (the settlement was already short of food) were attacked by native people. One, who returned with a dangerous wound, reported that the other had been wounded and carried away by his assailants. A search only turned up a shirt and a hat, 'both pierced with spears'. Phillip commented, 'There could be little doubt that the convicts had been the aggressors, though the man who returned strongly denied having given any kind of provocation.' Significantly, Phillip did not offer any evidence to support his contention that the convicts had been the aggressors. They might have been, or they might not have been. However, Phillip needed to believe that they provoked the assaults.

Phillip's attribution of the cause of the violence was so persuasive that it was repeated much later by David Dickenson Mann, a convict who arrived in the colony in 1799. Mann wrote,

> In vain did the governor issue order after order, and proclamation after proclamation; insults still continued to be offered to the natives, and such acts of retaliation ensued as circumstances would allow.

In a report to Lord Sydney dated 15 May 1788, Phillip reiterated that

> ...nothing less than the most absolute necessity should ever make me fire upon [the natives], and tho' persevering in this resolution has at times been rather difficult, I have hitherto been so fortunate that it never has been necessary.

On 30 May 1788, Phillip recorded that 'two men who had been employed in collecting rushes for thatch at some distance from the camp, were found dead'. He attributed the deaths to the fact that the men had stolen a native canoe. Worgan wrote that the men had been

> murdered in a most horrid Manner by the Natives, Three Points of Spears were taken out of one Man, two of which had Transfixed Him in the Back the Points sticking some Inches out of his Breast a large Piece of his Skull, including the Eye seemed to have been cut out with an Axe. In the other Man, no wound was discovered from Spears, but he appeared to have been struck with some heavy broad Weapon over his Face, as that Part was black and bloody.

He added that that it was the Governor's opinion that 'the Natives are not the Aggressors'.

Phillip set out to find the assailants and explain to them that the dead men had acted improperly and contrary to orders even though it was not clear which orders the two convicts had disobeyed. In his search for the assailants, 'after traversing the country more than twenty miles', they reached the north shore of Botany Bay. This was a long trek and showed how determined Phillip was to explain his point of view. Near Botany Bay, he met a large crowd of Indigenous men – Phillip wrote that there was no evidence that the aggressors were among them – all of whom were armed. Phillip recorded that he approached the group unarmed, at which the leading man in the group

> gave his spear away and met him with perfect confidence. In less than three minutes the English party found itself surrounded by more than two hundred men; but nothing occurred in this transaction which could in the least confirm the idea, that the natives were accustomed to act with treachery, or inclined to take any cruel advantage of superiority in numbers.

What Phillip failed to record was that although he was unarmed, he was backed up by armed men; and by this time, the Indigenous people knew the dangers of muskets very well.

During July 1788, Phillip noted that about twenty natives,

> armed with spears, came down to the spot where our men were fishing, and without any previous attempt to obtain their purpose by fair means, violently seized the greatest part of the fish which was in the seine... While this detachment performed this act of depredation, a much greater number stood at a small distance with their spears poized, ready to have thrown them if any resistance had been made.

He wrote that Indigenous people had formerly been satisfied with an arrangement by which fishing parties gave portions of their catches to them. This, wrote Phillip, was the only instance of which he knew where the natives had 'attempted any unprovoked act of violence', which he attributed to the fact that they were short of food.

Soon, Indigenous people increased their attacks on vulnerable Europeans. In trying to explain why this was happening, Phillip hit the nail on the head when he wrote, 'Their dislike to the Europeans is probably increased by discovering that they [Europeans] intend to remain among them...' However, once again he shied away from this uncomfortable line of reasoning and reverted to his former argument by portraying Indigenous people as reactors, not initiators, when he wrote that in all the cases where settlers had been attacked, 'there is great reason to suppose that in these cases the convicts have usually been the aggressors'. Phillip repeated this perspective in a dispatch to Lord Sydney dated 9 July 1788 when, describing the disappearance of a convict in the bush, he wrote, 'I have not any doubt but that the natives have killed him, nor have I the least doubt of the convicts being the aggressors.' However, as usual, in neither case did he provide evidence that the convicts had been aggressive.

At this stage, Phillip was avoiding putting two and two together to make four. Although he acknowledged that the settlers were causing distress by 'remaining among' Indigenous people – that is, by establishing a permanent settlement – he did not acknowledge that the Indigenous people were giving expression to their dislike by actively resisting colonisation. Phillip was still perpetuating the fiction that the Indigenous inhabitants were simple, tractable people who would accept 'whatsoever was offered'. For Phillip, it was a necessary fiction; if he admitted the truth, then hope of a policy of amity and kindness was at an end, and there was no possibility that 'a sanguinary temper was no longer to disgrace the European settlers'. Instead, he would have to accept that this was simply another instance of colonial oppression and indigenous resistance. To preserve his necessary illusions, the cognitively dissonant Phillip tried to delay acknowledging it for as long as possible. Perhaps he never did acknowledge it fully.

Eight months after settlement began, Phillip was still looking past, or denying, the obvious. In a dispatch to Lord Sydney dated 28 September 1788, Phillip reported that at Pittwater (which is about forty kilometres north of today's central Sydney) he and his party found 'about sixty of the natives, men, women, and children, with whom we stayed some hours'. Although they were friendly, stated Phillip, 'as I have ever found them, since they find we intend to remain, they appeared best pleased when we were leaving them'. Here he revealed a clear understanding of the situation, namely that, although Indigenous people might tolerate the Europeans as visitors, they did not want them to settle in their country. Reflecting on the encounter, Phillip wrote, 'it is not possible to say whether it was from fear or contempt that they do not come amongst us.' If fear, then fear of what? If contempt, then contempt for what?

A month later, in a dispatch to Lord Sydney dated 30 October, Phillip partially admitted the cause of the hostility when he wrote that the Indigenous people 'see no advantage' for the loss of 'that part of the harbour in which we occasionally employ the boats in fishing'. However, he did not acknowledge that the hostility was not only caused by the occasional loss of fishing grounds, but extended to uninvited settlement, to loss of ancestral country, and to ongoing encroachments on country.

Three weeks later, in a dispatch to Secretary Stephens dated 16 November 1788, Phillip wrote, 'The natives now avoid us more than they did when we first landed…' This behaviour suggested a concerted campaign by the groups around the Harbour. Again, Phillip reverted to his default explanation, namely that the reason was 'the robberies committed on them by the convicts'.

Two years after settlement began, in a dispatch to Lord Sydney dated 12 February 1790, Phillip still maintained the same position when he wrote that 'the natives having been robbed and ill-treated, now attack those [the convicts] they meet unarmed'.

Collins, who was deputy judge-advocate and lieutenant governor, believed that the Indigenous people 'by no means seemed to regard them [the colonists] as enemies or invaders of their country and tranquility'. (In other words, they welcomed colonisation!) Perpetuating the official line as Phillip's deputy, he would support Phillip's reasoning. Collins ascribed the worsening relations to the fact that the convicts were stealing Indigenous artefacts to sell to the sailors on the transport vessels, who also 'were procuring spears, shields, swords, fishing lines, and other articles from the natives, to carry to Europe; the loss of which must have been attended with many inconveniences to the owners…' While it was probably true that the convicts were acting provocatively by stealing artefacts, it would not have been the main reason for the hostility.

John Hunter, who succeeded Phillip as governor, reported the deaths of the rush-cutters (see earlier) as follows:

> It has been strongly suspected that these people had engaged in some dispute or quarrel with them (the native people), and as they had hatchets and bill-hooks with them, it is believed they might have been rash enough to use violence with some of the natives…

He, too, suggested that the convicts had instigated the clash, without providing proof of his assertion.

We see that, although Phillip occasionally cited other reasons for the violence between settlers and native people, such as land theft and loss of fish and fishing grounds, his consistent position was that it was sparked by improper actions by the convicts. Lieutenant-Governor Collins continued to support this view, for instance writing of the situation during early 1789 that 'had they [native people] never been ill treated by our people, instead of hostility, it is more than probable that an intercourse of friendship would have subsisted'.

The situation was exacerbated by the fact that the settlement began to suffer from a shortage of food within a few months of being founded. By late May 1788, only four months after arrival, Tench noted that fish, which had been plentiful, were now in short supply, and only the occasional kangaroo provided fresh food. The situation was so bad that 'the scurvy began its usual ravages, and extended its baneful influence, more or less, through all descriptions of persons'. It is not clear whether the shortage of food also affected the Indigenous people, although Tench's comment about the lack of fish suggests that this could have been the case. If so, the competition for scarce food would have intensified the Indigenous people's hostility toward the settlers.

Writing during September 1788, David Blackburn, ship's master, performed mental gymnastics to show that the Indigenous people were innocent of aggression, even when they were acting aggressively. Blackburn recorded that the convicts had been told that when they were in the bush they should not allow themselves to be isolated, nor to be in exposed positions. This was not happening; Blackburn wrote that

> Notwithstanding this order and precaution, however, a convict… having gone out with an armed party to procure vegetables at Botany Bay, straggled from them, though repeatedly cautioned against it, and was killed by the natives.

Blackburn noted that he had been killed with violence:

his head beat to a jelly, a spear driven through it, another through his body, and one arm broken.

The lesson that Blackburn drew from this incident was that

…every misfortune of the kind might be attributed, not to the manners and disposition of the natives, but to the obstinacy and ignorance of our people.

Deconstructed, Blackburn's argument was as follows: 1) for their own security, Europeans were ordered not to get into exposed or isolated positions; 2) Indigenous people only killed Europeans who disobeyed instructions and became easy targets; 3) therefore it was the victims' fault that they were attacked; it had nothing to do with 'the manners and disposition of the natives'. By implication, although the natives were naturally peaceable and accommodating, they would also savagely attack any European who was an easy target. This was equivalent to saying, 'The lions on the savannah are gentle and peaceful. However, if you walk around alone in the bush, the same lions will attack you and tear you to pieces.'

Were the natives peaceful, or were they aggressive? Blackburn suggested that they were both at the same time. This piece of mental gymnastics was another case of a person in a higher station refusing to acknowledge that the Indigenous inhabitants were aggressively defending their territory. Any excuse would do, rather than face up to the fact that the colonists were not welcome in Indigenous country.

By November 1788, Blackburn had changed his mind. Now, without giving a reason for his about face, he wrote that the Indigenous people 'in all probability will always look upon us as enemys and take all advantages in their power'.

To return to Phillip's view of relations with the Indigenous people: no matter how conciliatory he was, his underlying aim was always to bring them into voluntary subjection, with the emphasis on subjection. He justified his project in terms of bringing civilisation to the savages. While he admitted that civilised life did have the disadvantage of giving rise to artificial wants, its greater advantage was that it would 'confer upon them [Indigenous people] benefits of the highest value and importance' by teaching them how to clothe their bodies and how to shelter from the cold and wet. Also, it would give them 'the means of procuring constant and abundant provision.' (He wrote this even though the colony was suffering from a severe shortage of food!) In this regard, Phillip wrote to the home secretary, Lord Sydney, on 5 July 1788 as follows:

> I hope…to be able to persuade some of them [Indigenous people] to live near us and every possible means shall be used to reconcile them to us, and to render their situation more comfortable. At present I think it is inferiour to that of the beasts of the field…

The civilising mission was the colonisers' main justification for their project. Once again, we find this in Tench's words when he described the departure of the First Fleet from Cape Town on its journey to Botany Bay:

> we weighed anchor, and soon left far behind every scene of civilisation and humanised manners, to explore a remote and barbarous land; and plant in it those happy arts, which alone constitute the pre-eminence and dignity of other countries.

Although Tench did not say what he meant by humanised manners and the happy arts, he was confident that planting them in the new land would greatly benefit the native people. Underlying Tench's words was the assumption that it was the responsibility of civilised people to impart their values and way of life to savages, who would benefit greatly from becoming civilised. The end justified the means.

Although Hunter was conciliatory in the matter of the death of the rush-cutters, he was less inclined in that direction than Phillip. For instance, when he was exploring parts of the harbour in a small boat during August 1788, a group of natives beckoned to him to come ashore. He suspected that the natives only wanted the Europeans to come within reach because they thought that they did not have firearms. Without hesitation, Hunter produced his musket and aimed a shot at the natives. When his gun misfired, one of his companions let fly with small shot. Hunter concluded by saying that he was bewildered at this 'treacherous' behaviour, because he was sure that he and his party had done nothing 'hostile or mischievous' to warrant it. He wrote that Indigenous people were 'exceedingly terrified by fire-arms'.

During November 1788, Hunter wrote that the native people displayed 'a more than ordinary degree of hostility' after they had 'murdered some of our people'. In saying that the Indigenous people initiated the violence, Hunter now differed from Phillip who, as seen above, still maintained that Indigenous people only reacted to provocations from the settlers.

However, Hunter was still 'wholly at a loss to guess' why the native people were hostile and reasoned that it was all because a lack of communication. He wrote,

> I am inclin'd to think, that by residing for some Some time amongst or near them, they will soon discover that we are not their Enemys, a light in which they no doubt Considerd us on our first arrival.

Further, it was his opinion that 'much of this hostile disposition in them towards us' would be prevented if only they could communicate with an Indigenous person 'who from a habit of living amongst us' could act as a mediator or go-between. (Mediator and go-between are my words, not Hunter's.) In short, Hunter believed that the colonisers' aims and intentions were honourable and commendable, and that they would be accepted as such if only the Indigenous people could understand the situation.

Between January 1788 and October 1788, when Bradley sailed to the Cape of Good Hope for supplies, his attitude toward the Indigenous people changed considerably. As already noted, in Botany Bay, Bradley described how 'the Boat Crews amused themselves with dressing the Natives with paper and other whimsical things to entertain them'. This was comparatively innocent, free of violence and threats, as was the desire of the Indigenous men to know whether the clean-shaven sailors were men or women. As Bradley described it, one of the Indigenous men showed a sense of fun when the sex of the sailors had been clarified. The man 'ran in amongst the Bushes, made himself a Belt of Grass and came dancing out with it round his waist with leaves hung over it…' At this point, Bradley's only criticism was that the local people stole any piece of cloth that they could lay hands on.

Soon after settlement began, Bradley was also happy to report that two stragglers had been kindly treated by the local people. He wrote,

> Two of the Seamen on the North shore straggling into the woods without Arms or any thing to protect themselves sailor like, met with some Natives, Men, Women and Children who very friendly, met them without fear and eagerly accepted of a Jacket which one of the Sailors gave them, they were all entirely naked.

A few days later, when Bradley was with a party in a boat, at South Head they 'were cordially received by 3 Men'. The Europeans went ashore and 'while our people were cooking the dinner, the natives were amongst them playing, looking at the Boat, manner of Cooking etc. and were without any weapons the whole time…' However, by March 1788, only six weeks after settlement began, Bradley was recording aggressive behavior by local people, as follows:

A seaman who had been missing for some days was found] stript of all his clothes, not able to stand and scarce sensible. (10 March)

Some of the Natives came to a place where a party of the Convicts had been left to cut rushes and finding them unarmed wanted to steal their tools, being opposed they threw their Spears at the Convicts. (16 March)

Captain Meredith up the Harbour met several of the Natives on the land opposite to Dawes Island, they were very familiar and had many things from him, but after he left them, droping his boat along the shore, a spear was thrown that passed near him. (20 March)

Two of the Convalescent Convicts were sent out to get greens for the Hospital, they were met by a party of the Natives about a mile from the Camp, the Natives attack'd them, first by throwing stones which they were returning when they used their spears. One of the Convicts escaped with a barbed spear broke in him entering at the small of the back and was obliged to be cut out, he reported that the other Convict was killed and that the Natives had stript him and taken the body away with them. (22 May)

Two convicts who were cutting rushes were found dead: One of them had 3 Spears in him and one side of his head beat in. (30 May)

The Governor's fishing boat, met a great number of the Natives in the lower part of the Harbour, as they were hauling the Sein, the People gave fish to all the Natives, but they were not satisfied with that, they closed upon the people employed in the Boat and took what they pleas'd, their Musquet happening to be left in the Boat. (10 June)

By the time that he wrote the latter entry, Bradley had concluded that the Indigenous people only attacked unarmed people. Also, although Bradley did not say it, there was a sense that the Indigenous people were distinguishing between authority figures, such as officers, toward whom they were not aggressive, and other ranks, including convicts, toward whom they were aggressive when it was safe to be so. By October 1788, Bradley stated forthrightly that

Latterly they have attack'd almost every person who has met with them that has not had a musquet and have sometimes endeavoured to surprise some who had.

Agreeing with Hunter, Bradley concluded, 'The Musquet now seems to be the only thing to keep them in Awe…'

Tench was more forthright in his description of relations between the two parties. During October 1788, he wrote, 'Unabated animosity continued to prevail between the natives and us…' This, wrote Tench, was 'similar to the vindictive spirit which Mr. Cook found to exist among their countrymen at Endeavour River, they more than once attempted to set fire to combustible matter, in order to annoy us.' Here, to suit his narrative, Tench misconstrued the events at Endeavour River. In the first place, after a period of caution, at Endeavour River several Indigenous men had established friendly contact, to the extent of coming on board the ship. Secondly, the aggression that led to the firing of grass at Endeavour River had been caused by the fact that the Europeans had taken turtles that belonged to the Indigenous people.

Further, while lauding the efforts that the settlers, inspired by the governor, had made to establish friendly relations with the natives, in a fit of petulance and frustration, Tench attributed failure to

> the fickle, jealous, wavering disposition of the people we have to deal with, who, like all other savages, are either too indolent, too indifferent, or too fearful to form an attachment on easy terms with those who differ in habits and manners so widely from themselves.

The fault for the lack of friendly relations was all on the side of the Indigenous people, who were afraid to get to acquainted with people who were different to them.

While people in higher stations were more strategic and analytical in their attitudes toward the Indigenous people, the lower ranks were less nuanced. Jacob Nagel, an ordinary seaman, wrote truculently that when he and his fellows were out fishing in a small boat, the governor 'would not Allow us Arms to defend our Selves for fear we Should kill sum of them [Indigenous people] in our Own defence'. His attitude towards the native people was unreflective and condescending. When Phillip gave one of the Indigenous people a looking glass, Nagle described the incident as follows:

> he Admired it equal to a monkey he would look in it and put his hand to the back of it to feel the person he Saw.

The man then indicated that he would like some of the fish that was cooking in a pot. When Nagle, who anticipated that the man would not have experience of boiling water, invited the man to take some,

> he very Readily put his hand into the Boiling Water to take Out of the fish but to his great Asstonishment he gumped he Run he hollowed and away to his Cannoo put his hands in the Water then padded it is Impossible to discribe the Anticks he Cut we Laughing…

A few days later, after they had been 'Robed of Our School of fish', one of the natives approached them in a canoe. Nagle and his fellows recognised him as one of the robbers and got their revenge by persuading him to ignite cartridge powder in his hand. Nagle described the sequel as follows:

> the flame Smoke and Burning his hand and flying in his face he gave a Spring and a hollow that I Never saw equalled and Run to his Cannoo and put off sometimes paddling with One hand and then the Other Untill he got to the Other Side the Laughture and Noise Alarmed the Sarjent…

Nagle's opinion was that 'The Natives here Are the Most Misserables on the See Coast I ever Saw.'

Ralph Clark, who was promoted to the rank of lieutenant of the Marines during his time in the colony, shared Nagel's unfavorable opinion of the Indigenous people. During November 1788, he wrote,

> they are a Set of Savage Rascals for they will take the Advantage of the defencesles where the[y] can Such of the convicts that the[y] meet in the woods but as for a Red Coat the[y] will not come near

them upon no Account what ever the[y] are So much affraid of fire Arms.

Nagle and Clark give us insights into the attitudes of the majority of the settler population, namely convicts, ordinary soldiers, and seamen. Nagle wrote that 'It was Always the goveners Studdy to Cultivate & Naturelise those Natives as Much as possible…' There was little reason why those in lower stations, including Nagle, should identify with the strategy that was being pursued by the governor and his circle.

Earlier, I noted that both Phillip and Hunter bemoaned the lack of communication with the Indigenous people. Their view was that friendly intercourse (Phillip's words) and the intercession of a mediator would bring about understanding that would dissipate the hostile attitude of Indigenous people toward the settlers.

What exactly was to be communicated to the Indigenous people? Phillip wanted the local people to understand that the settlers would treat them with amity and kindness if only they would submit to the new authority. As Phillip put it, his aim was 'to bring even the native inhabitants of New South Wales into a voluntary subjection; or at least to establish with them a strict amity and alliance'. Regarding voluntary subjection, it is not clear why Phillip thought that Indigenous people would voluntarily relinquish their sovereignty. This was wishful thinking. The second course, 'amity and alliance', could not be pursued while the settlers were encroaching on Indigenous territory and resources. In short, how would even the most effective 'communication' convince the Indigenous people that the colonisers were offering a good deal? In fact, it is likely that communication would only have confirmed their worst suspicions about the intentions of the newcomers, namely that they were there permanently, and that their demand for land and resources was insatiable.

Also, as ever, the aim was to civilise the natives by teaching them to wear European clothing, become agriculturists, settle individually on plots of land, convert to Christianity, and live in houses with roofs and walls, along with other aspects of European culture. As Phillip wrote in a dispatch dated 10 July 1788 to Lord Sydney, every means shall be used to reconcile them to live amongst us, and to teach them the advantages they will reap from cultivating the land...

Hunter continued the theme of convincing the native people that the Europeans had kindly intentions when he explained that an interlocutor was needed because 'the Governor having found that no encouragement he cou'd give them [the native people] woud dispose them to Visit the Settlement of their own accord', the governor had decided to kidnap someone to provide the medium of communication.

Towards the end of 1788, Tench also wrote that, in exasperation at 'this state of petty warfare and endless uncertainty', the governor had decided to capture some of the local people. The result, wrote Tench, would be that either (1) the action would 'inflame the rest to signal vengeance, in which case we should know the worst and provide accordingly' (in other words, matters would be brought to a head and there would be a showdown), or (2) the captives would give a favourable report to their fellows, namely that they had been treated with 'mildness and indulgence'. Presumably, this would encourage their fellows to abandon their aggressive behaviour. Tench wrote that 'intercourse' with captives also 'promised to unveil the cause of their mysterious conduct, by putting us in possession of their reasons for harassing and destroying our people...'

On 31 December 1788, two boats set off for Manly Cove with instructions to capture some local people. After a friendly interaction with a party of Indigenous men on the beach – Tench wrote that they 'were enticed by courteous behaviour and a few presents to enter into conversation' – the landing party suddenly seized two men. There was a vigorous struggle, during which one man escaped and the other was hurried away in a boat. Although the rest of the men fled when the attack began, the cries of the prisoners drew them back, and soon the Europeans were assailed with missiles. Tench recorded that their assailants only withdrew when many shots had been fired over them.

The incident was traumatic for all concerned. Hunter wrote that the terror this poor Wretch [the captive] Sufferd can better be conceiv'd than Expressed, He believe'd he was to be immediately Murderd, but upon the Officers coming into the Boat, they remov'd the rope from his Neck to his Leg, treated him with so much kindness, that he became a little more Chearfull…

(Hunter was absent from the settlement between September 1788 and May 1789, so he was reporting what he was told later.)

At the settlement, the captive, Arabanoo, was shackled with a leg iron. By the following day, he appeared to understand that he was not in imminent danger. After joining the senior personnel at the governor's table for New Year's dinner, Tench recorded that Arabanoo 'dined heartily on fish and roasted pork…' after which he 'Stretched out on his chest, and putting his hat under his head, he fell asleep'. Next, Phillip decided to display Arabanoo to his fellows to convince them that he was unharmed. In a boat, they lay off the beach where Arabanoo had been captured. When Arabanoo saw some of his fellows, wrote Tench, 'he was greatly affected, and shed tears'. The people on the beach asked Arabanoo why he did not escape by jumping overboard and swimming to the shore, but 'He only sighed, and pointed to the fetter on his leg, by which he was bound'.

Tench recorded an ironic episode involving Arabanoo. When some convicts were sentenced to be flogged for instigating a clash when they tried to rob Indigenous people, Phillip required Arabanoo to witness the punishment so that he would understand that depredations against Indigenous people would not be tolerated. Ironically, Arabanoo, who was a member of a race that the settlers termed savage, reacted to the floggings with 'disgust and terror only'. (This resonates with Tench's description of the reactions of a group of Indigenous people who, about two years later, were required to watch a convict being 'severely flogged' for stealing Indigenous artefacts. Tench wrote, 'There was not one of them that did not testify strong abhorrence of the punishment and equal sympathy with the sufferer.')

Later, Arabanoo was unshackled and, apparently reconciled to his situation, or perhaps apprehensive about how he would be received by his fellows, he lived at large in the settlement until he died of smallpox during May 1789. Hunter wrote about Arabanoo that 'every person in the Settlement were Were much Concernd for the loss of this man'.

Although Arabanoo taught Phillip and his colleagues something about Indigenous culture and customs – what, or how much, is not known – the plan failed completely. Tench wrote,

> By his [Arabanoo's] death, the scheme which had invited his capture was utterly defeated... The same suspicious dread of our approach, and the same scenes of vengeance acted on unfortunate stragglers, continued to prevail.

In short, more than a year after settlement began, the Indigenous people were as suspicious and hostile as ever.

Three
Nature's night

During the early years of contact, how did the settlers view and describe the Indigenous people? The letters, journals and reports did not necessarily speak for the 'settlers' as a group, because most were written by privileged men who had similar social positions as 'gentlemen' and were predominantly of the officer class. (Some writers use the term 'officer period' to describe these journals and correspondence.) They were 'gentlemen' who enjoyed 'superiority' by benefiting from what Tench termed 'the fortuitous advantage of birth'; he wrote,

> Let those who have been born in more favoured lands and who have profited by more enlightened systems…recollect that by the fortuitous advantage of birth alone they possess superiority…

He added, 'untaught, unaccommodated man is the same in Pall Mall as in the wilderness of New South Wales'. Most of the 'common people' of the First Fleet, such as convicts, sailors and enlisted soldiers, would have fallen into Tench's category of 'untaught, unaccommodated man'.

The writers of the 'officer period' were different from those who followed them in one important respect, namely that the influence of the Enlightenment made them intensely curious about Indigenous people – that is, they desired to explore, to investigate the unknown, to describe it and to place it within explanatory frameworks or schemas. In some cases, they framed and shaped their writings for readers at home – some of their publications were also widely read in European countries – who shared similar interests and outlooks. Also, as with all publicity-conscious authors, they knew that drama, sensation and exotica added to the impact of their texts.

Many of the commentators also shared a characteristic that was seldom found in later colonial writings, namely, they saw Indigenous people as individuals, and not just as representatives of a type. For instance, there are extensive, almost rounded, portrayals of characters such as Arabanoo, Bennelong, Barangaroo and Gooreedeeana. Also, there are reports of interactions that involve humour, poignancy, sympathy and compassion. For all the deliberations on 'savagery' and 'primitiveness', often there was an attempt to 'understand' and to engage with the strange culture and its people. As an example, here is Tench's description of the reactions of two Indigenous women who were among a group of their fellows who were required to watch a convict being flogged for stealing Indigenous artefacts:

> There was not one of them that did not testify strong abhorrence of the punishment and equal sympathy with the sufferer. The women were particularly affected; Daringa shed tears, and Barangaroo, kindling into anger, snatched a stick and menaced the executioner. The conduct of these women, on this occasion, was exactly descriptive of their characters. The former was ever meek and feminine, the latter fierce and unsubmissive.

The stolen artefacts belonged to Daringa.

As males and 'gentlemen', the observers identified with a top-down and hierarchical society, in which power was wielded by the monarch, by hereditary nobles and by a parliament that was elected from a rich and privileged section of the population. Almost all power-wielders were male, while almost all females, no matter their age or status, were dependents. Also, power was highly centraliszed. A 'flatter' society without superiors and inferiors, and without inherited wealth and power, together with the supposed 'responsibility' and 'duty' that went with it, was regarded as a recipe for anarchy.

Most members of the British ruling class, and those within their orbits such as the 'officer class', would have agreed with Edmund Burke who wrote in 1790,

I should therefore suspend my congratulations on the new liberty of France [that is, the French Revolution] until I was informed how it had been combined with government; with public force; with the discipline and obedience of armies; with the collection of an effective and well-distributed revenue; with morality and religion; with the solidity of property; with peace and order; with civil and social manners.

Applying Burke's 'formula' for a well-functioning society to Indigenous society and culture as viewed through the eyes of the colonial commentators, there was no perceptible legal system such as a written body of laws, law courts, lawyers, law-enforcement officers or prisons; there were no armies; there was no system of taxation and collection of public revenue; and property was not privately owned. Also, Indigenous people did not have only one, fixed abode; rather, within the limits of their territory, they moved from place to place as seasons and resources dictated.

In addition, as will be seen, most of the commentators doubted that the Indigenous people had a religion; therefore, it was also doubtful that they had moral sense.

Finally, although the Indigenous people did appear to preserve 'peace and order', their means of doing so were regarded as odd and even barbarous.

Burke's criterion of 'civil and social manners' entails a huge range of behaviours. 'Civil' would entail 'civility', such as politeness, courtesy, respect and showing regard for others, while 'manners' would entail accepted ways of behaving in company so as not to cause offence and, therefore, would include behaving in ways that were appropriate to one's class, sex, age and position. Clearly, 'civil and social manners' are strongly located in culture, gender and time/period. For instance, the colonial commentators were amazed and affronted by the habitual nakedness of Indigenous people, and most of all by female nakedness. This was a time when wealthier people in Europe wore elaborate and stylised costume that exaggerated gender distinctions, while even 'common people' wore clothing that covered most parts of the body, except for the lower arms and, sometimes, décolletage. Headgear was common.

Indigenous nakedness attracted a lot of attention and was usually equated with 'savagery' and 'primitiveness'. For instance, King wrote the following about his first acquaintance with Indigenous females:

> we saw a great number of Women and Girls with infant children on their shoulders, make their appearance on the beach, All *in puris naturalibus pas meme la feuille de figeur* [completely naked, without even a leaf to cover themselves] – those natives who were round the boats made signs for us to go to them, and made us understand their persons were at our service; however I declined this mark of their hospitality.

It is striking that King described the females' nakedness in a mixture of Latin and French. This resonates with the use of the same languages for some erotic or risqué passages in English texts of the eighteenth and nineteenth centuries, presumably to show the writer's distance from the 'distasteful' material, and/or possibly to restrict accessibility only to 'gentlemen' who would have the education and breeding to be able to handle the material responsibly. Also, by referring to a leaf as a covering for nakedness, he was evoking the Biblical tale in which Primal Man and Woman were, paradoxically, both innocent and sinful. However, the Europeans could only view Indigenous nakedness through postlapsarian lenses.

When one of the women came alongside the boat, apparently thinking that King had invited her for sexual congress, he instead used a handkerchief to cover that part of her body 'where Eve did ye Fig leaf...' At this, 'the Natives then set up another very great shout and my female visitor returned on shore'. Was it a cry of astonishment? Probably. An invitation to sexual congress had been declined and, instead, the woman's nakedness had been covered with a handkerchief. These were two very different cultures, indeed.

Although King's account of the encounter with a woman who was offering herself for sexual congress has been accepted on his terms, it may be asked whether his interpretation of the incident was correct. I say this because it was completely out of keeping with all other encounters between settlers and Indigenous people during the early years, when women and children were kept out of sight. Also, there is no other record of Indigenous women publicly offering themselves for sexual congress. In other words, the incident was one of a kind. Was King so overcome by the sight of nubile, female nakedness that he misinterpreted the incident? Was it his culture-bound assumption that any woman who appeared naked before men had to be an erotic object? We don't know.

Phillip associated nakedness with a lack of civilisation when he wrote that the natives were 'in so rude and uncivilized state as not even to have made an attempt towards clothing themselves…' Because they seemed to be adversely affected by cold weather and rain, he was convinced that they would find clothing useful, 'if they could be induced to come enough among the English to learn the use of it'. Further, Phillip was suggesting that the Indigenous people were so 'undeveloped' that they did not even have the concept of clothing; they would have to learn about it from the settlers. Anticipating the need that would arise, Phillip wrote to Lord Sydney,

> Cloathing for the natives, if sent out, will, I daresay, be very acceptable to them when they come amongst us. I should recommend long frocks and jackets only, which will equally serve both men and women.

Clothing on the European pattern and style was an essential element of the colonial project to civilise the natives. If they did not need it in their 'natural' state, then they should be taught to need it.

Worgan described the Indigenous people as 'Children of Nature' – 'nature' being a pejorative term that denoted 'uncultivated', 'undeveloped', 'crude', and even 'sinful' or 'pre-redemption'. We see this attribute of 'nature' in a stanza of Charles Wesley's hymn, 'And Can It

Be', written in 1738, where 'nature' connotes 'sin' and 'night' (that is, darkness, ignorance and despair) while spiritual revelation and redemption are symbolised by light and release from the 'chains' of sin and 'nature's night':

> Long my imprisoned spirit lay / Fast bound in sin and nature's night; / Thine eye diffused a quickening ray, / I woke, the dungeon flamed with light; / My chains fell off, my heart was free, / I rose, went forth, and followed Thee.

Consistent with the view that the Indigenous people were in a state of nature, Worgan described Indigenous women at Botany Bay as 'these curious Evites' and 'as naked as Eve before she knew Shame'. The latter phrase displays ambivalence. Were they innocent, in a prelapsarian state, or were they unredeemed savages who were mired in depravity and sinfulness? The latter view predominated; the consensus was that the Indigenous people would benefit by being 'developed' so that they would be elevated out of their primitive and savage state.

All commentators agreed that the Indigenous people were 'savages'. Tench wrote that

> they certainly rank very low, even in the scale of savages. They may perhaps dispute the right of precedence with the Hottentots or the shivering tribes who inhabit the shores of Magellan. But how inferior do they show when compared with the subtle African; the patient watchful American; or the elegant timid islander of the South Seas.

He also wrote that 'a less enlightened state…can hardly exist'. This was confusing because, as seen earlier, Tench ranked the African people of the east coast of South Africa as 'the most savage set of brutes on earth' – yet here, when grading savagery, he placed the 'subtle African' far above the Indigenous Australian. Who was more 'savage', the African or the Indigenous Australia? Tench's ranking system seemed to be unstable. However, one thing was certain: Europeans were on the top rung.

Regarding civilisation and Indigenous savagery, Tench produced a flight of purple prose when he wrote that he often wished that 'European philosophers whose closet speculations exalt a state of nature above a state of civilization' – here, too, 'nature' was contrasted with 'civilization' – could realise the truth about 'the phantom' that they had imagined. If they did so, 'Possibly they might then learn that a state of nature is, of all others, least adapted to promote the happiness of a being capable of sublime research and unending ratiocination.' Savages did not have the developed capacities for investigation, reasoning, and research. Here, Tench opposed a state of 'nature' to the cultivation and exercise of logic and reason. The erring philosophers would realise, wrote Tench, that the reality was that a savage was 'a creature deformed by all those passions which afflict and degrade our nature, unsoftened by the influence of religion, philosophy and legal restriction'.

Sublime research, unending ratiocination and philosophical deliberations about nature compared to civilisation: these were Enlightenment values and concerns. It is doubtful that even one-twentieth of Tench's countrymen fitted the bill, because formal education, and even literacy, were only enjoyed by a small proportion of society.

Bradley had no doubts about ranking when he wrote that the Indigenous people of New South Wales 'are Certainly the Lowest Class of Human beings'.

In agreement with these views, soon after settlement began, Phillip wrote that although little was known about the Indigenous people, he did not think that there was much to learn because these were people 'among whom civilization and the arts of life have made so small a progress'.

A specific instance of the primitive nature of the Indigenous people was the deficiency of their language in which, claimed Tench, they could not 'count with precision more than four', although they could count as far as ten by holding up the fingers of both hands. Everything beyond that was 'great' or 'great-great'. This limitation, said Tench, caused 'their computations of time and space to be very confused and incorrect'.

Collins also asserted that because they could not count beyond three or four, they could 'have no regular computation of time'.

Further evidence of the primitive nature of Indigenous people was found in the fact that they were hunter-gatherers rather than cultivators. Bradley characterised their means of subsistence as living 'chiefly on fish, Berrys and the fern Root and Where they find most Oysters or the best fishing, there they take up their Residence in the Hollow of A Rock till they have Cleard the Neighbouring Rocks of the Oysters and other small shell fish'. He noted, 'We never met with the smallest appearance of any kind of Cultivated ground.' Tench claimed that, although 'suffering from the vicissitudes of their climate, strangers to clothing, though feeling the sharpness of hunger' and although their food supply was 'precarious,' they were nevertheless 'ignorant of cultivating the earth'. Phillip noted that 'notwithstanding the goodness of the soil it is a matter of astonishment how the natives, who know not how to avail themselves of its fertility, can subsist in the inland country'. He added that whereas the sea provided food for those who lived at the coast, in the case of those who lived inland, he could not believe that 'with their spears, the only missile weapon yet observed among them, they should be able to procure any kind of animal food'. He added that the country inland – he was referring to the upper Hawkesbury region – was 'so good and so fit for the purposes of cultivation' that he planned to send settlers there as soon as possible.

Bowes thought that although Indigenous people sometimes ate kangaroos, they were 'too stupid and indolent a set of people to be able often to catch them'.

Collins provided a trenchant opinion of the quality of the land and its inhabitants when he wrote of 'a land where wretchedness, want, and ignorance have laid their iron hands on the inhabitants, and marked with misery all their days and nights'. He also wrote that the Indigenous people were 'revengeful, jealous, courageous, and cunning'. Phillip thought that they were 'perfectly honest' among themselves and gave as proof that they often left their spears and other implements on the beaches, in full confidence that they would not be stolen. Tench stated, 'I do not hesitate to declare that the natives of New South Wales possess a considerable portion of that acumen, or sharpness of intellect, which bespeaks genius.' However, their negative qualities were levity, fickleness, and 'their passionate extravagance of character'. He noted that although they were 'indeed sudden and quick in quarrel', they were not 'implacable' in revenge.

Watling had nothing good to say about the character of Indigenous people. He wrote, 'Irascibility, ferocity, cunning, treachery, revenge, filth, and immodesty, are strikingly their dark characteristics – their virtues are so far from conspicuous, that I have not, as yet, been able to discern them.' He also wrote, 'they seem also in many other respects to be capable of much improvement; but they are so very unsteady and indolent'. Watling, a convict who arrived in the colony on 7 October 1792, one year after Bennelong led native people into the settlement, might have had close-up experiences of Indigenous people. If so, we don't know what those experiences were, to produce such an unfavourable opinion.

Almost all descriptions of the appearance, physique, and constitution of the Indigenous people were positive, as reflected in the name, 'Manly', that Phillip gave to a part of the Harbour where he was impressed by the 'manliness' of the inhabitants. Hunter's description of their physical appearance is typical:

> The Men in general are from 5 feet 6 inches to 5 feet 9 high, are thin but very straight and Cleanmade, Walk very erect and are active, the Women are not so tall nor so thin, but are generally well made.

Tench and Collins noted that there were few instances of deformity, and Collins specifically noted that 'Their sight is peculiarly fine…' Hunter commented that they had very good teeth.

The commentators also noted the healthy constitutions of the Indigenous people. For instance, Tench wrote,

Their excellent habit of body, the effect of drinking water only, speedily heals wounds without an exterior application which with us would take weeks or months to close…Their native hardiness of constitution is great.

He also recorded that when a party of settlers, Tench included, went westward to explore the country, they were accompanied by two Indigenous men, Colbee and Boladaree. Although the Europeans were exhausted after the first day of traipsing over broken country, the two Indigenous men were still fresh. Tench wrote,

> Our fatigue to-day had been excessive; but our two sable companions seemed rather enlivened than exhausted by it. We had no sooner halted and given them something to eat than they began to play ten thousand tricks and gambols. They imitated the leaping of the kangroo; sang, danced, poised the spear and met in mock encounter.

Collins wrote that Indigenous people 'Possess by nature a good habit of body…'

How was it that the Indigenous people were so healthy and robust, if their diet was so poor, and if they had so much difficulty subsisting? None of the commentators noted or addressed this contradiction.

There was general distaste for the fact that the Indigenous people seldom seemed to wash or clean their bodies. For instance, Hunter wrote,

> they are abominably filthy, they never Clean their Skin, it is generally Smeard with the fatt of such Animals as they kill, and coverd with every sort of dirt, sand from the Sea beach, and the ashes from their fires, all adhere to their greasy skin which is never Wash'd.

He also said that

> their hair is short, strong and curly, but they seem to have no Method of Cleaning or Combing it, it is therefore filthy and matted.

Bradley commented, 'they are very dark and keep their skins so dirty that it is hard to tell the true colour of them, their hair is clotted with dirt and full of vermin, and as they never wash themselves unless by chance or accident, the beauty which many of them from regularity of features and pleasing countenances would be allowed to have, is destroyed,' while Tench objected to 'the rank offensive smell'. Collins, while agreeing that 'the oil, together with the perspiration from their bodies, produces, in hot weather, a most horrible stench', explained that they did this 'as a guard against the effects of the air and of mosquitoes, and flies; some of which are large, and bite or sting with much severity'.

Most commentators noted that girls and women were missing two joints from the little fingers of their left hands. No one could explain this practice until Collins wrote that 'at last' he had learned 'that these joints of the little finger were supposed to be in the way when they wound their fishing lines over the hand'. Regarding male ornamentation, it was widely noted that, in Hunter's words,

> Some of the Men wear a piece of Wood or bone thrust thro' the Septum of the Nose which by raising the opposite sides of the Nose, widens the Nostril & spreads the lower part very much…

In addition, most men had their right front upper tooth removed which, as Collins explained at length, was done as part of an elaborate initiation ceremony for young men.

Phillip wrote that

> The inhabitants of New South Wales have very few ornaments, except those which are impressed upon the skin itself, or laid on in the manner of paint.

Ornamental scarring was popular with both men and women, while some commentators provided vivid and detailed descriptions of the body painting that was done for ceremonial occasions. For instance, Tench wrote,

> Some are streaked with waving lines from head to foot; others

marked by broad cross-bars, on the breast, back, and thighs, or encircled with spiral lines, or regularly striped like a zebra. Of these ornaments, the face never wants its share, and it is hard to conceive any thing in the shape of humanity more hideous and terrific than they appear to a stranger – seen, perhaps, through the livid gleam of a fire, the eyes surrounded by large white circles…

The subjects of women and relationships between the sexes attracted interest. The writers' curiosity was piqued by the fact that girls and women remained concealed during early encounters, apart from occasional exceptions such as King's encounter at Botany Bay. For instance, soon after settlement, Hunter reported the following incident while he and a boat party were exploring a remote part of the Harbour:

Whilst we were Employ'd with this party [of Indigenous men], we Observ'd at a distance a Number of their Women, who were peeping from their Concealments, but durst not gratify their Natural Curiosity by appearing before and Conversing with us.

Similarly, commenting on the situation during the first two years of settlement, while the Indigenous people of the Harbour area remained aloof, Bradley noted that 'no one in the Colony' had had sexual relations with an Indigenous woman. He continued that he did not know what conventions the women observed in such matters; however, in all encounters,

the Women are kept at a distance when we do not come unawares upon them, and a guard with several lances always ready for their protection has been usually found.

The colonial commentators wrote at length about how the men treated the women. Collins spoke for all when he wrote that the women's condition was 'wretched' and that they were 'mere slaves of the men'. He wrote that the men beat the women so frequently and so harshly that

We have seen some of these unfortunate beings [women] with more scars upon their shorn heads, cut in every direction, than could be well distinguished or counted.

Phillip's opinion was that

> in general they [women] are observed on this coast to be much less cheerful than the men, and apparently under great awe and subjection. They certainly are not treated with much tenderness…

Similarly, Tench, who was much taken by a young woman named Gooreedeeana (see later), was sorry to find that her head was 'covered by contusions and mangled by scars'. In addition, she showed him a wound on her leg which, she said, had been caused by a spear that had been thrown at her by a man who had dragged her by force from her home 'to gratify his lust'.

Courtship and marriage customs attracted considerable attention. Describing how marriages were initiated when different groups got together at dances, Tench wrote,

> Courtship here, as in other countries, is generally promoted by this exercise, where every one tries to recommend himself to attention and applause.

To gain favour, men took the initiative and approached women with gifts. However, other commentators only described how men seized women by force to carry them off as wives. Collins described the process at length and with relish:

> Is it not shocking then to think that the prelude to love in this country should be violence? …the poor wretch is stolen upon in the absence of her protectors; being first stupified with blows, inflicted with clubs or wooden swords, on the head, back, and shoulders, every one of which is followed by a stream of blood, she is dragged through the woods by one arm…the lover, or rather the ravisher, is regardless of the stones or broken pieces of trees which may lie in his route, being anxious only to convey his prize in safety to his own party, where a scene ensues too shocking to relate.

According to Collins, the members of the woman's clan did not take revenge for the abduction, while the woman soon settled down as a member of her husband's tribe.

Despite describing an orderly pattern of courtship, Tench also related how a man would carry out 'an attack upon the chastity of some neighbouring fair one' and would drag her away. This would be the signal for war; the men of the two groups would engage each other violently:

> they discharge their spears at each other, and legs and arms are transpierced. When the spears are expended the combatants close and every species of violence is practiced. They seize their antagonist and snap like enraged dogs, they wield the sword and club, the bone shatters beneath their fall…

As seen, there was a disparity in the accounts that were provided by Collins and Tench. Did 'abduction' result in revenge-taking, or did it not? Or were there other factors at play that neither commentator comprehended?

Despite the distaste that they expressed for dirt, grease and lack of ablutions, there was appreciation for the charms of the younger women. Collins wrote that although the black, bushy beards and nose bones of the men made them 'disgusting', the women had a 'feminine delicacy' and, although they were habitually naked, 'they sought with a native modesty to conceal by attitude what the want of covering would otherwise have revealed'. He continued by saying that they often reminded him of 'The bending statue which enchants the world' (that is, the Venus de Medici), and then added, perhaps by way of excusing his too-appreciative gaze, 'though it must be owned that the resemblance consisted solely in the position'. Tench stated that if Indigenous men portrayed the charms of their women, they would draw them as 'the "Venus aux belles fesses" [Venus of the beautiful buttocks]'.

To deflect attention from their evident appreciation of Indigenous female charms, both Collins and Tench illustrated the subject with reference to classical statues, while Tench further distanced himself, and emphasised his delicacy on the matter, by using French to refer to the physical feature that attracted him. This reminded me of Moodie (see earlier) who, as a 'gentleman' and a British visitor, cast a sardonic and supercilious eye over much that he saw in the Cape Colony during his visit in the 1830s but was clearly attracted by the indigenous Khoisan ('Hottentot') women. He wrote, 'It may seem somewhat extraordinary to Europeans, but it is nevertheless true, that the colonists, both Dutch and English, are very partial to the female Hottentots.' (Moodie, being a 'European' and not a 'colonist', would not be susceptible to this attraction…!) Of course, wrote Moodie, the colonists concealed their fancies from their wives by pretending to be disgusted by Hottentot women. Moodie continued by saying, 'The colonial female Hottentots, indeed, are often strikingly elegant in their proportions, and they have all that lightness, and ease in their motions for which all savages are remarkable.' It was no wonder, wrote Moodie, that 'they are often preferred to the clumsy, torpid, and insensible Dutchwomen, with their stony eyes and jealous domineering manners'. Here, Moodie tried to divert attention from his own attraction to the indigenous women by transferring attention to the colonists.

Tench provided a comprehensive tribute to Indigenous female charms when he described Gooreedeeana, who was Bennelong's sister. He wrote lyrically,

> She excelled in beauty all their females I ever saw. Her age about eighteen, the firmness, the symmetry and the luxuriancy of her bosom might have tempted painting to copy its charms.

He praised her mouth, her teeth, and her face ('distinguished by a softness and sensibility') and called her 'an elegant timid female'. Proceeding to intimacy, he examined her head

> to learn whether the attractions of Gooreedeeana were sufficiently powerful to secure her from the brutal violence with which the women are treated.

Not so: as cited above, he discovered 'with grief' that her head was severely scarred.

Tench said that he only saw Gooreedeeana once more, when she and some other women were in a canoe near the mouth of the harbour.

This time, 'She was painted for a ball, with broad stripes of white earth, from head to foot, so that she no longer looked like the same Gooreedeeana.' Tench and his companions obviously tried to get close to her because, to avoid their 'eagerness and solicitude to inspect her', she moved away 'and acted the coquet to admiration'.

Tench was also taken by the charms of Bennelong's wife, Barangaroo. He wrote,

> ...she behaved so well, and assumed the character of gentleness and timidity to such advantage, that had our acquaintance ended here, a very moderate share of the spirit of travelling would have sufficed to record, that amidst a horde of roaming savages, in the desert wastes of New South Wales, might be found as much feminine innocence, softness, and modesty (allowing for inevitable difference of education), as the most finished system could bestow, or the most polished circle produce.

Collins declared that for Indigenous women,

> Chastity was a virtue in which they certainly did not pride themselves; at least, we knew women who, for a loaf of bread, a blanket, or a shirt, gave up any claim to it, when either was offered by a white man; and many white men were found who held out the temptation.

He described how 'several girls' acted as prostitutes, 'passing the night on board of ships' and being paid for their services. Further, he noted that they had learned that Europeans disapproved of nakedness and 'many of them [were] extremely reserved and delicate in this respect when before us; but when in the presence of only their own people, perfectly indifferent about their appearance.'

Once again, wearing (European) clothing was associated with being 'reserved and delicate', while nakedness was associated with being indifferent.

Although Collins was a meticulous recorder of events, his comments about the behaviour of Indigenous women reflected a time when local Indigenous people had entered a new phase by moving into the settlement. There, they had to adopt a different lifestyle, including finding different ways of getting their livelihoods. Probably, prostitution was an exigency, not a traditional practice.

Indigenous religion attracted attention, as was to be expected in an age when Christian orthodoxy, the Anglican Church, and conventional worship were as much mainstays of the state as class divisions, the monarch, and the law. For instance, Phillip's commission included this injunction: 'And it is further our royal will and pleasure that you do by all proper methods enforce a due observance of religion and good order among the inhabitants of the new settlement…' Also, individual and national 'morality' were inseparable from religious belief – and those who held to the 'only' true religion, namely Protestant Christianity that was preferably of the Anglican persuasion, had the 'best' morality.

The consensus was that the Indigenous people did not have any religion. Blackburn's opinion was that 'they are the only people I Ever heard of who did not worship Some Deity; It is pretty Clear they do not' while Hunter's opinion was 'Neither ye Sun, the Moon, or the Stars seem to take up or occupy more of their attention, than they do that of any of the other Animals which inhabit this immense Country.' Collins agreed, stating that these were the only people anywhere who had 'no trace of religion'.

Initially, Tench wrote that the Indigenous people 'do not appear to observe any kind of religion'. However, he modified his opinion later, stating that it was his 'firm belief that the Indians of New South Wales acknowledge the existence of a superintending deity'. He changed his mind because he observed that they had certain superstitions about natural phenomena, such as weather events and the positions of planets and stars which, he concluded, 'conveys a direct implication of superior agency'.

In connection with religion, several commentators discussed superstitions among Indigenous people, providing examples such as a 'carrahdy' treating a sick man (Collins termed the procedure 'a farce') and a woman who fell ill because she believed that she had been cursed by other women. Tench made the connection between religion and superstition by writing,

> He who believes in magic confesses supernatural agency, and a belief of this sort extends farther in many persons than they are willing to allow.

Considerable attention was given to burial customs, which some commentators described in detail. Burial customs were juxtaposed with religion, although no conclusions were drawn.

Writers gave a lot of space to aspects of material culture, such as weapons, hunting and fishing gear, and other common articles. In addition, almost as much space was given to types of shelter, to foodstuffs, and to the preparation of food for eating. Some descriptions gave a lot of attention to the materials from which implements and utensils were made, as well as to the methods by which they were made. This is not surprising: not only would readers in Britain and Europe find these details 'exotic', but they would also inform the market that existed for Indigenous artefacts. Tench alluded to this when he wrote,

> As very ample collections of all these articles are to be found in many museums in England, I shall only briefly describe the way in which the most remarkable of them are made.

Despite all that was written about Indigenous people during the early years, there was one issue that was hardly addressed – and it was by far the most important one, if Europeans were to 'understand' Indigenous people. That issue was the 'world view' of Indigenous people. World view is a broad, catch-all term that embraces the set of beliefs, values and (largely) unreflective practices that underpin and guide a society. A shared world view makes a community or society out of a collection of individuals.

There were several reasons why the commentators did not attempt to acquire this level of understanding. One reason was the fact that there was almost no meaningful contact with Indigenous people during the first two years of settlement. Another reason was that when closer contact did take place, it was on European terms within the bounds and authority of the colonial settlement (see later). A third reason was that the Europeans were confident in the superiority of their culture and, rather than trying to understand the Indigenous world view, sought to elevate the native people from 'savagery' by imposing European 'civilisation' on them. As Tench wrote about Indigenous people, 'Their form of government, and the detail of domestic life, yet remain untold. The former cannot occupy much space.' Although little was known, in the opinion of the writers, there was little to know.

The closest that anyone came to addressing the organisation of Indigenous society was when Collins stated, 'Without distinctions of rank, except those which youth and vigour confer, theirs is strictly a system of "equality"…' He added that this produced one 'inconvenience', namely that 'the strong triumph over the weak'. He also wrote, 'They disclaim all idea of any superiority that is not personal…', by which he meant that authority was not inherited and did not derive from family, tradition or heritage.

Here, I want to comment on Collins's statement that a system of 'equality' was one in which 'the strong triumph over the weak'. Was he implying that the contemporary British system, in which wealth and power were inherited and in which the great majority of the population was uneducated, occupationally and socially restricted, and without political power, was not one of strong over weak? Probably, in view of Collins's position and background, he would have portrayed the system as a benevolent one, in which a minority of wise and altruistic people ruled over the undeserving but appreciative majority, like an eighteenth century embodiment of Plato's 'guardians'.

Collins also touched on, but did not understand, an essential aspect of Indigenous 'law', namely the role of the elders as custodians of knowledge and lore. He noted that whenever an elder came into town, Indigenous people 'impressed us [the colonists] with an idea that we were looking at persons to whom some consequence was attached even among the savages of New Holland.' He also noted that members of 'the tribe of Cameragal', which was one of the clans that Phillip identified, were given special respect because they were 'most numerous, had the best fishing grounds, and perhaps had suffered less from smallpox'. However, it looks as if Collins confused clan status with respect that derived from exceptional knowledge and standing in 'law'. In fact, Collins and all other commentators completely missed two essential organising principles of Indigenous society, namely the composition of a 'clan' and the allocation of authority, as explained by William Buckley (in Morgan, 1852):

> ...the tribes are divided into families: or rather, I should say, composed of them – each tribe comprising from twenty to sixty of them. They acknowledge no particular chief as being superior to the rest; but, he who is most skilful and useful to the general community, is looked upon with the greatest esteem...

Apart from an initiation ceremony that Collins witnessed and wrote about at length, the other aspect of customary behaviour to which he gave attention was justice via restitution for injury. He described at length how the accused had to defend himself against being speared.

None of the commentators even touched upon the existence and significance of 'Dreaming', sacred places and their relationship to Dreaming, or the special responsibility that Indigenous people felt to care for, and not over-extend or misuse, the resources of 'country'.

Even the best-intentioned Europeans would have had difficulty understanding the Indigenous world view, because a huge gulf separated the two cultures in almost every significant aspect. For instance, European culture was hierarchical, while Indigenous culture was 'flat'; European culture was literate, while Indigenous culture was oral; Europeans believed in 'development' and exploited natural resources, altering and dominating the environment, while Indigenous people cared for 'country' and lived within the resources that the land provided; Europeans associated 'productivity' with economic activity and output, while Indigenous people lived off the land; Europeans owned property and had fixed abodes, while Indigenous people were semi-nomadic within their boundaries; European societies had fixed, demarcated boundaries, while, to quote Powell and Hesline, for Indigenous people, 'Conscious connection was generally focused externally, on complex links to others…' and Europeans associated spirituality with monotheism and belief in a god who, paradoxically, was both loving and vengeful, while Indigenous spirituality was associated with the ancestors and Dreaming.

When describing Indigenous people, the early commentators were like a man laboriously peeling an onion, but only up to a certain point: although he removed many layers, he did not get anywhere near the core. This resonates with Knapman's (2017) observation that 'Manners and customs represented the highpoint of Enlightenment discourse on civilisation.' He continued that describing manners and customs fell short of 'a deeper understanding of peoples, one which went to their very core, beyond the idea of civilisation'.

Four
April 1789 to 1790: wretched natives

During April 1789, Hunter, who had just returned to the settlement after a long voyage, wrote that 'the Smallpox had made its appearance a few Months ago amongst these poor unfortunate Creatures [Indigenous people]'; he continued that it was

> truly Shocking to go round the Coves of this Harbour which were formerly so much frequented by the Natives, where in the Caves of the Rocks which us'd to shelter whole familys in bad Weather, were now to be seen, Men, Women, & Children laying dead...

He noted that until then, during the first fifteen months of colonisation, neither the settlers nor the native people had been affected by smallpox.

Tench wrote that boat parties reported 'finding bodies of the Indians in all the coves and inlets of the harbour...' while Bradley stated that the epidemic had caused such 'dreadful havock' that no Indigenous people were to be seen anywhere in the Harbour area. Many unburied bodies had been found, some 'with a child laying dead close to them and some who have apparently used their utmost exertions to get at water, having been found laying dead between a Cave and a run of Water'. Collins corroborated, writing that boat parties reported that 'the bodies of many of the wretched natives of this country' were to be found 'either in excavations of the rock, or lying upon the beaches and points of the different coves...'

Nobody could explain how or why the disease had broken out. Tench listed the following possibilities. 1. 'Is it a disease indigenous to the country? 2. 'Did the French ships under Monsieur de Peyrouse introduce it?' (However, as Tench noted, the French ships left Botany Bay more than one year earlier.) 3. 'Had it travelled across the continent from its western shore, where Dampier and other European voyagers had formerly landed?' 4. 'Was it introduced by Mr. Cook?' 5. 'Did we [that is, the First Fleeters] give it birth here?' Supplementing the latter question, Tench added that 'No person among us had been afflicted with the disorder since we had quitted the Cape of Good Hope, seventeen months before.'

Tench noted a further possibility, namely that the virus could have been spread deliberately. Although he acknowledged that the First Fleet's surgeons 'had brought out variolous matter in bottles', he dismissed the idea, saying, 'to infer that it was produced from this cause were a supposition so wild as to be unworthy of consideration'.

Subsequently, some observers have claimed that the disease was spread deliberately. They have pointed out that European colonisers used smallpox as a weapon of biological warfare against indigenous people in other parts of the world. For instance, it is accepted that the British spread smallpox among native Americans via blankets that they distributed in Quebec during 1763. However, while it is possible that the colonial authorities at Port Jackson did spread smallpox deliberately, there is no proof that they did.

The smallpox brought about an outpouring of sympathy and concern by the colonial commentators. Hunter wrote that any person who showed symptoms of the disease was

> immediately deserted by their friends, and left to perish in their helpless situation for want of Sustenance, some have been found Sitting on their haunches with their head reclind between the knees, others leaning against a rock with the head resting upon it…

He also noted that two Indigenous children, a boy and a girl, both suffering from the disease, were brought to the hospital for care, together with two older men who were probably their fathers. Although the men died, the children survived. The boy, Nabaree, and the girl, Abaroo, were adopted into settler families.

Tench provided a more detailed account of the events involving the boy. He wrote that when 'intelligence was brought that an Indian family lay sick in a neighbouring cove', the governor, accompanied by Arabanoo and a surgeon, went to the place immediately. There they found the boy pouring water over the head of a supine old man while 'near them lay a female child dead, and a little farther off, its unfortunate mother…' Tench wrote that they were in a very poor condition: 'the body of the woman shewed that famine, superadded to disease, had occasioned her death: eruptions covered the poor boy from head to foot; and the old man was so reduced, that he was with difficulty got into the boat.' They were so weak that 'they quietly submitted to be led away'.

Tench continued that 'an uninhabited house, near the hospital, was allotted for their reception, and a cradle prepared for each of them'. Although the man was so weak that he could take nothing but water, the boy eagerly accepted some fish, which he cooked and ate. Both patients were bathed, clothed and put to bed. Arabanoo attended to them and reassured them that they were safe from harm.

The ravages of disease not only allowed displays of amity and kindness but also brought some Indigenous people into involuntary submission. Nor were the settlers' motives disinterested; Hunter wrote that

> thro the means of these Children if they retain their Native language, a more intimate and friendly intercourse with the people of this Country may in time be brought about.

Collins expressed the same idea, writing that it was important to save the lives of smallpox sufferers 'as the knowledge of our humanity, and the benefits which we might render them, would, it was hoped, do away the evil impressions they had received of us'. A catastrophe for the Indigenous people was an opportunity for the colonial administration to demonstrate its humanity and beneficence.

During July 1789, while a colonial party was exploring Broken Bay, the Hawkesbury River and adjoining coastal areas, some of its members encountered an Indigenous woman who was weak from smallpox. Hunter, who described her as 'a poor Young Creature who…was very Weak, and unable from a Swelling in one of her Knees to get off to any Distance', devoted considerable space to recounting how he and his companions ministered to her. The woman, who was left behind on the beach when her companions fled at the approach of the boat, tried to conceal herself in long grass which, wrote Hunter, was 'very Wett and I shou'd have thought very uncomfortable to a poor Naked Creature'. Hunter continued that she had 'Crept off and Conceald herself in the best manner she cou'd amongst the grass' and was so terrified when a hunter fired a gun near her hiding place 'that she Cried out and discovered herself'. Governor Phillip, always eager to display his benevolent intentions towards Indigenous people, led a group to the place where 'this poor Miserable Girl' lay. Pathetically, she tried to cover 'her Naked body over with the Wett grass'; further, wrote Hunter, 'She was very much frightened on our approaching her, and Shed many tears with piteous lamentations.' Although the Europeans did not understand what she was saying, they 'felt much Concern at the distress she seem'd to suffer, [and] endeavour all in our power to make her easy…'

The officers ordered sailors to make a fire to keep her warm. Also, they provided her with birds and fish to eat, and water to drink, 'of which she seem'd to be much in want'. That night, before the explorers retired to sleep nearby, they provided the woman with more firewood and dry grass. Next morning, reported Hunter, the woman seemed to be less fearful. When she called to her friends, who were concealed nearby, Hunter imagined that she was letting them know 'that the Strangers were not Enemys but friends…'

That evening, continued Hunter, they visited the woman again. Hunter wrote, 'with her was a female Child about two years Old and as fine a little Creature of that Age as I ever saw…' The woman 'was laying with her Elbows & Knees on the ground covering the Child from our sight with her body, probably to shelter it from the Weather but I rather think on account of its terror…' When they spoke to her, wrote Hunter, 'she rais'd herself up and sett on the ground with her Knees up to her Chin and her heels under her, and was at that Moment I think the most Miserable spectacle human shape [*sic*] I ever beheld.' After improving the covering of her hut against the weather, again they supplied her with birds, fish, firewood and fresh grass. Hunter was sure that by now the woman understood that the Europeans 'had nothing in View but her Comfort…' Next morning, after providing the woman with fresh supplies, they took their leave and proceeded with their expedition.

It is significant that Hunter who, as a senior official, was party to the governor's plans for Indigenous people, wrote about this encounter at length and provided exhaustive details about the attention that they gave to the suffering woman. His purpose was to convince himself, his colonial peers and his readers that the settlers were kind-hearted and well-intentioned.

People in 'higher stations' were kind and sympathetic toward Indigenous people, partly out of instinct ('noblesse oblige') but primarily because it was politic and self-justifying. However, they only extended kindness and sympathy towards weak and helpless Indigenous people, and/or towards those who were in their power. Independence, resistance, and assertiveness did not wear well with them.

It has been estimated that the smallpox killed between fifty and ninety per cent of the Indigenous people in the Harbour area. In a dispatch to Lord Sydney dated 13 February 1790, Phillip wrote that 'one-half of those who inhabit this part of the country died'. He based this estimate on information received from Bennelong.

Collins's graphic words captured the disaster:

> The number that it [smallpox] swept off, by their own accounts, was incredible. At that time a native was living with us [that is, Arabanoo]; and on our taking him down to the harbour to look for his former companions, those who witnessed his expression and agony can never forget either… He lifted up his hands and eyes in silent agony for some time; at last he exclaimed, 'All dead! all dead!' and then hung his head in mournful silence.

The epidemic spread far beyond the Harbour area. For instance, the woman who was assisted by Hunter and his colleagues was found about forty kilometres from Port Jackson, while Tench reported that they found many Indigenous people suffering from smallpox near present-day Richmond, which is about sixty kilometres from the centre of modern-day Sydney. The swift passage of the disease is shown by the fact that both observations were made during June 1789, only about two months after the outbreak was first reported. In the dispatch of 13 February (as above), Phillip wrote that the disease 'must have been spread to a considerable distance, as well inland as along the coast. We have seen the traces of it wherever we have been.' One reason for the swiftness of the transmission was that, as Collins said, the few survivors 'had fled up the harbour…'

Testifying to just how widely the disease spread, Petrie observed that some old Indigenous men bore pockmarks when he and his family settled in what is now Brisbane in 1839. The men said that the disease had ravaged their community long before the first white people arrived in the region, which was in 1823. Sydney and Brisbane are about 900 kilometres apart.

The epidemic also played a part in initiating a radical change in the relationship between Indigenous people and the settlers in the Harbour region. Soon, the 'communication' that Phillip and others so much wanted was taking place regularly. However, this did not happen immediately. At the time of Arabanoo's death during May 1789, Tench noted that nothing had changed: he wrote,

> By his death, the scheme which had invited his capture was utterly defeated…The same suspicious dread of our approach, and the same scenes of vengeance acted on unfortunate stragglers, continued to prevail.

A year later, during April 1790, the situation was the same; Blackburn wrote,

> As to the natives, we are almost as ignorant of their particular man-

ners and customs (if they have any) as we were at first. They will not come among us though every method has been used to invite them.

Nevertheless, less than a year later, during March 1791, Hunter wrote, 'the Natives being now become very familiar and intimate with every person in the Settlement….' What happened to change the situation so drastically?

One factor would have been the ongoing pressure on Indigenous land and resources that was caused by the expansion and demands of the colony, and another factor would have been the smallpox epidemic. This catastrophe – its suddenness, its reach, its dreadful nature and its inexplicable origin – must have had far-reaching effects on the ways in which the survivors viewed their culture, their internal and external relationships, and their place in the world.

In the absence of direct evidence, it is useful to look at comparable incidents elsewhere. One illuminating event is the 'Great Cattle Killing' of the Xhosa people in the eastern region of today's Eastern Cape Province in South Africa during the 1850s. (From colonial times until 1994, this region was called 'the Transkei'.) The killings were inspired by a prophetess who said that she had visions that the ancestors would arise and lead a force to drive out the white people if people were obedient and killed all their cattle. After mass killings of cattle and destruction of crops during a period of three years, by 1857 about 40,000 people had died.

The event exacerbated fault lines in indigenous African society, with deep divisions emerging between 'Believers' (largely 'traditionalists') and 'Unbelievers' (many of them influenced by Christian missionaries). Also, with destitution everywhere, large numbers of Xhosa people left their tribal lands and entered the colony where, starving and defenceless, they were yoked into settler society as serf-like labourers. In time, with the fabric of society severely damaged and the size of their territory drastically reduced, many Xhosa men became low-paid migrant labourers on the mines and other industries while traditional tribal lands, often located in less fertile areas, became overcrowded and impoverished 're-serves'.

There are striking similarities between the condition of the Xhosa people at the time that the Cattle Killing began, and the condition of Indigenous people in the Harbour area during the first years of colonisation. In both cases, there was a devastating disease. In the case of the Xhosa, it was lung sickness, which was unwittingly imported from Europe and infected large numbers of settler-owned and Xhosa-owned cattle. Like many African groups, the Xhosa had a deep regard and affection for their cattle, which represented wealth and success, and were tokens of a healthy society. The disease was both an economic and cultural catastrophe. Also, like smallpox, the lung sickness epidemic caused deaths that were painful, distressing and unsightly, which exacerbated the effect. In both cases, the epidemics could not be explained; they were like visitations by angry, vengeful, supernatural forces, or like an 'an infernal visitation' as Mann described the effects of the smallpox on the Indigenous inhabitants. He continued,

> …its effects are such as to justify this idea, in some degree, for it seldom fails to desolate and depopulate whole districts, and strews the surface of the country with the unburied carcases of its wretched and deserted victims.

Also, as with the Indigenous people of the Harbour area, the South African catastrophe occurred while colonial advancement was depriving the indigenous people of their land and resources. Some Xhosa groups were forced to intrude on others, which caused tensions and insecurities for all concerned. In summary, in both the Australian and South African cases, traditional society was doubly stressed, first by colonial pressures and then by devastating illness and deaths.

The 'Herero Genocide' of 1904–1907 in Namibia (then German South West Africa) provides another case of indigenous people who, after being felled by disaster, looked to the culture and beliefs of the oppressor. This happened after the Germans defeated the Herero 'rebellion' and pursued a policy of genocide, as proclaimed by the German commander-in-chief, General Von Trotha – namely, 'Any Herero found inside the German frontier [that is, within German South West Africa], with or without a gun or cattle, will be executed. I shall spare neither women nor children…' Gewald described how the majority of the 'Camp Herero' – that is, the captives in the 'concentration camps' – converted to Christianity, because it not only promised an improvement in their material conditions, but also offered the prospect of a means of social organisation that was beyond German control, as well as the promise of salvation.

Further, regarding the aftermath of the 'Herero Genocide', Steinmetz wrote,

> Ovaherero converted in great numbers to Christianity in the concentration camps after resisting missionary blandishments for more than a half century. Many Ovaherero men began to wear odd bits of German military uniforms. These practices emerged out of the post-1904 context of defeat, identification with the aggressor, and German 'native policies' that emphasized an abject form of partial assimilation which turned Ovaherero survivors into isolated proletarians.

The same was true in Australia, where the vanquished Indigenous people, such as survived, were expected to accept the dominant, colonial culture, while serving as serf-like labourers for the new owners of the lands that they had once called 'country'.

Colonialists always exploit existing fault-lines in traditional societies as well as cultivating new ones. In *Things Fall Apart*, the Nigerian novelist Chinua Achebe showed this process at work. The central character, Okonkwo, was socially and financially ambitious, physically strong, brave in war, and had risen from poverty to wealth through his own endeavours. He equated tenderness, kindness, thoughtfulness and sympathy with weakness because he identified these 'weak' qualities with his musically gifted and unambitious father, whom he despised. In reaction, Okonkwo always wanted to be thought of as 'strong'.

However, Okonkwo's son, Nwoye, was sensitive, tender-minded, and reflective. He was badly shaken when a boy who lived in their household for three years as a hostage to the village, and with whom he had a close relationship, was killed by the men of the village. To make matters worse, Okonkwo took part in the killing to affirm his manly qualities, even although an elder advised him not to be involved because 'that boy calls you father'. Also, Nwoye began to question other cruel practices, such as the perplexing tradition of exposing twins to die in the forest.

When the Christian missionaries began to work in Igboland, Nwoye was among the first to join the new religion. Achebe wrote,

> It was not the mad logic of the Trinity that captivated him. He did not understand it. It was the poetry of the new religion, something felt in the marrow. The hymn about brothers who sat in darkness and in fear seemed to answer a vague and persistent question that haunted his young soul – the question of the twins crying in the bush and the question of Ikemefuna who was killed. He felt relief within as the hymn poured into his parched soul.

Achebe showed that one way that Christianity gained influence was by accepting the weakest and most marginalised people into its ranks: 'They were mostly the kind of people that were called efulefu, worthless, empty men.' The Christians also prospered by flouting local customs and surviving unscathed, which called into question ancient tradition and suggested that a new, more powerful force was impacting on Igboland: 'it became known that the white man's fetish had unbelievable power'.

Soon, an elder foretold the cultural dislocation that was approaching, saying,

> I fear for you young people because you do not understand how strong is the bond of kinship. You do not know what it is to speak with one voice… An abominable religion has settled among you. A man can now leave his father and his brothers. He can curse the gods of his fathers and his ancestors, like a hunter's dog that sud-

denly goes mad and turns on his master. I fear for you; I fear for the clan.

Another elder said that the colonial administration 'has put a knife on the things that held us together and we have fallen apart'.

However, as Achebe showed, many people appreciated the wealth and opportunities that came with it. Achebe wrote,

> The white man had indeed brought a lunatic religion, but he had also built a trading store and for the first time palm-oil and kernel became things of great price, and much money flowed into Umuofia.

It ended badly for Okonkwo. After he and other elders were arrested and humiliated by the colonial administration, Okonkwo urged violent resistance. When the divided community would not support him, he killed a colonial official and hanged himself in despair, rather than face colonial justice. The novel concludes with the colonial district commissioner reflecting that the story of Okonkwo's fate would contribute an interesting paragraph to the book that he was writing, which was titled *The Pacification of the Primitive Tribes of the Lower Niger*.

Although the events in Igboland and Sydney Harbour were half a world apart and separated by about a century, there were strong similarities. In both cases, there was the invasion of a colonial power with no respect for Indigenous autonomy and culture. In both cases, the invaders touted superior weaponry and technology. In both cases, the invaders undermined indigenous confidence and self-esteem by riding roughshod over traditional boundaries and customs while remaining unscathed, and even profiting by the violations. In both cases, wealth and esteem could be gained by associating with the colonialists.

With Governor Phillip still wanting to capture some Indigenous people to replace Arabanoo as a medium of communication, Bradley recorded two abortive attempts. On the first occasion, during August 1789, a boat containing the boy Nabaree went 'about the Harbour' to try to convince some of the native people to enter the settlement voluntarily. Ironically, the mission misfired because 'the boy was much inclined to join the naked tribe'. Later that month, they made another failed attempt. Bradley reported that 'they met with several [native people] in the North Arm and found them very friendly, they did not take much notice of the Native boy who accompanied the Party'. Significantly, this encounter also took place in the Middle Harbour area.

During both encounters, the Indigenous people were friendly, if wary, which suggests that their attitude towards the settlers was ameliorating.

During November 1789, a boat party managed to seize two men at Manly Cove. Nagle, who was in one of the boats, wrote that 'the Govener had a design of taking Sum of the heads of the Natives to Natrulise them'. Nagle also said that 'the(y) Ware the head Warriers of those tribes'; here, Nagle gives details that are not found elsewhere, regarding the men's status and the use of the plural 'tribes'.

Bennelong (also called Wollewarre, Boinba, Bunde-bunda, and Wogetrowey) and Colbee were taken to the settlement, where they were shackled and guarded, but were otherwise treated 'indulgently'. Colbee soon escaped but Bennelong was prevented from doing so and remained in the settlement for six months.

Five
The West is let in

The following timeline forms a framework for this chapter:
April–May 1789: the smallpox epidemic killed a large proportion of the Indigenous inhabitants of the Harbour area.
May 1789: Arabanoo died of smallpox, leaving no Indigenous adult within the colonial settlement.
May 1789–September 1790: Indigenous hostility towards, and avoidance of, the settlers continued.
November 1789–May 1790: Bennelong was captured, lived in the settlement, and then escaped.
June–July 1790: The settlement continued to expand: a new town was laid out at Rose Hill (Parramatta), about twenty-five kilometres from central Sydney, and five ships arrived, bearing more than 1,000 convicts, officers, and men of the newly raised New South Wales Corps, together with desperately needed provisions and stores.
7 September 1790: Governor Phillip was speared at Manly.
September 1790: a few days after the spearing, Bennelong and others conversed with some colonial officers. They were told that the governor was recovering and would not seek retribution for the attack.
8 October 1790: Bennelong and three companions visited the settlement and were well received. Other visits followed.
November 1790: 'our greatest source of entertainment now lay in cultivating the acquaintance of our new friends, the natives'. (Tench)

During the period between the smallpox epidemic and the end of the year, 1789, there was no change in the hostile attitude of the Indigenous people. In fact, Bradley recorded five occasions on which there were aggressive actions against settlers. Four of the incidents were in the Middle Harbour area, while one was described as occurring in a 'lower cove', which was probably in the same area. Bradley said that about fifty Indigenous men participated in one attack, while 'a great number of Natives' participated in another incident.

Apart from showing that hostilities were continuing, the incidents are significant for two reasons. From the number of people involved, it looks as if the survivors of the epidemic had formed a new group, or groups, that bridged the former clan boundaries. Collins confirmed this when he wrote,

> Bennillong told us, that his friend Cole-be's tribe being reduced by its effects [that is, the smallpox] to three persons…they found themselves compelled to unite with some other tribe, not only for their personal protection, but to prevent the extinction of their tribe.

Here, it is useful to discuss the 'distribution' of Indigenous people in the Harbour region, pre-smallpox.

In a dispatch to Lord Sydney dated 13 February 1790, Phillip provided the following information:

- About the north-west part of this harbour there is a tribe which is mentioned as being very powerful, either from their numbers or the abilities of their chief…the tribe is named Cammerragal…
- From the entrance of the harbour, along the south shore, to the cove adjoining this settlement…the tribe Cadigal…
- The south side of the harbour from the above-mentioned cove to Rose Hill, which the natives call Parramatta…the tribe, Wanngal.
- The opposite shore…the tribe, Wallumedegal.
- The other tribes which live near us are those of Gweagal, Noronggerragal, Borogegal, Gomerrigal, and Boromedegal.

Phillip's classification of 'clans' or 'tribes' in the Harbour region has endured. For instance, the Wikipedia entry (accessed 9 July 2019) for 'Eora' stated,

Eora is used specifically of the people around the first area of white settlement in Sydney. The generic term Eora generally is used with a wider denotation to embrace some 29 bands. The sizes of bands, as opposed to clans, could range from 20 to 60 but averaged around 50 members. -gal denominates the clan or extended family group affixed to the place name.
- Cammeraygal. (Port Jackson, North Shore, Manly Cove)
- Wanegal. (South of the Parramatta River. Long Cove in Rose Hill)
- Cadigal. (South side of Port Jackson)
- ('Snapper fish clan'. North of the Parramatta River. Milson Point, North Shore opposite Sydney Cove).

Other clans listed in the entry are the Walumedigal, Burramattagal, Bidjigal, Norongeragal, Borogegal, Karegal and Gweagal.

As can be seen, Phillip's classification of 1790, and the Wikipedia classification of 2019, are almost identical.

There is some scepticism about Phillip's classification. In the first place, there are questions about how much the colonists knew, and what they knew about Indigenous society and structure. For instance, in the same dispatch (13 February 1790), Phillip wrote,

> …[Bennelong] lives with me, and will soon be able to inform us of their customs and manners, but of which at present I can give your Lordship very little information.

The colonists' information about the Indigenous people, sketchy as it was, must have come from Arabanoo and Bennelong. However, it was admitted that Arabanoo did not speak English well, and that little was learned from him. Also, as seen, Phillip admitted that, at the time that he wrote, they had not learned much from Bennelong. This was corroborated by Blackburn, who wrote two months later (during April 1790), 'As to the natives, we are almost as ignorant of their particular manners and customs (if they have any) as we were at first.'

Other writers also commented on the imperfect nature of the communication between Indigenous people and the Europeans. Thomas Watling, a convict who arrived during October 1792, asserted that the colonists had little command of the Indigenous language. He wrote, 'Glossaries have been attempted by some of our pretending and aspiring gentry, who, I am conscious, are as much ignorant of it as myself.' (Watling probably wrote this during 1793.) It might be thought that, as a convict, Watling had little acquaintance with what the colony's 'pretending and aspiring gentry' knew or did not know. However, he was a competent artist who was much better educated than the average run of convicts; also, because of his artistic ability, he was well acquainted with John White, the surgeon, and probably also with David Collins, the judge-advocate. Further, three years later in September 1796, Collins wrote,

> Language, indeed, is out of the question; for at the time of writing this nothing but a barbarous mixture of English with the Port Jackson dialect is spoken by either party; and it must be added, that even in this the natives have the advantage, comprehending, with much greater aptness than we can pretend to, every thing they hear us say.

There is further reason for scepticism because Phillip showed that he misunderstood, or made unfounded assumptions about, significant aspects of Indigenous society when he wrote in the same dispatch, 'The natives live in tribes, which are distinguished by the names of their chief, who probably takes his name from the district in which he resides.' Firstly, there were no 'chiefs' in Indigenous society, in the sense of ordained or inherited authority. Instead, there were different loci of authority – for instance, there were leaders for warlike activities, there were respected elders for law, and there were custodians of different aspects of what is called 'women's business' and 'men's business'. Many loci of authority transcended the 'band' or 'clan' and were only exercised at large gatherings. Secondly, there is no evidence that prominent Indigenous people took their names from the districts in which they resided.

Even if Phillip's 'snapshot' of demarcated territories and discrete identities was correct, the situation altered drastically within a short time as things became much more fluid, when old boundaries and identities, if they had ever existed, disappeared.

Phillip remained the only authority on the distribution of Indigenous people in the Harbour area partly because, whether his classification was accurate or not, no one with access to pen and paper had any interest in questioning or amending his views. After all, Phillip was the boss, and he wielded almost unlimited power within the colony. Higher authority in London was far away – exchange of correspondence took at least one year – and in any case, London gave almost unqualified support to its man in New South Wales.

In summary, for someone who had 'very little information', Phillip produced a surprisingly confident and detailed classification of 'tribes', their domains and aspects of their organisation.

There is doubt about Phillip's classification for at least two more reasons. The first is that there appears to have been a lot of linguistic misunderstanding between the British commentators and their Indigenous informants. For instance, Powell and Hesline (2010) suggested that the name 'Wangal' for Bennelong's 'tribe' reflected misunderstanding. They proposed that Bennelong was asked (in English) 'Where do you belong?' and simply translated the question itself by replying, 'Won gal?' Hearing this, someone recorded that he belonged to the 'Wangal' tribe. (That is, they recorded that he belonged to the 'Where-do-you-belong-tribe.') Powell and Hesline gave examples of similar misunderstandings to suggest that this hypothesis was not far-fetched.

They also observed that

> The notion of tribal entities, so favoured by the British, did not necessarily feature prominently in Aboriginal preoccupation and identity… The core of Aboriginal coalescence, the extended family grouping, was so small it mandated marriage beyond the band. Conscious connection was generally focused externally, on complex links to others preferred above any possible inward-looking clan identity.

Further, they stated that the European concern with tribes reflected 'nascent ideas of European nationalism…coupled with an Enlightenment obsession with naming and classifying' and that 'the British persisted in their imposition of a notion of "tribes" derived from their North American experience and elsewhere.'

Europeans also imposed the idea of tribes in their colonies for easier manipulation and control. For example, in Namibia (colonial German South West Africa) at the beginning of the German colonial period, there were several 'Herero' groups, spread over central Namibia. Although they were closely linked by several factors, such as origin, culture, belief and language, each was an autonomous polity with a recognised chiefly line, and there was no 'paramount chief' of the Hereros. However, during the 1890s, the German governor, Leutwein, set about creating a paramount chief by elevating Samuel Maherero, the chief of the central Herero group, who could easily be manipulated for various reasons, including the fact that his capital town and territory were conveniently close to the seat of German authority in Windhoek. By incorporating Samuel Maherero into his wars and oppressive activities against the other chiefs – for instance, Leutwein had Maherero participate in a 'court martial' that passed the death sentences on two rival chiefs – within a short time, Leutwein succeeded in establishing him (Samuel Maherero) as the recognised 'paramount chief' of the 'Herero'.

Leutwein's strategy was the common one of 'divide and rule', because he realised that he was militarily weak and could not withstand attacks by combined forces of indigenous people.

In the Harbour area, notwithstanding evidence to the contrary, the British authorities continued to view the Indigenous people through the tribal prism. For instance, on 4 January 1817, the *Sydney Gazette* reported that at Parramatta, at the instigation of Governor Macquarie, there had been an assembly of 'Native Tribes' at which 'the chiefs were placed on chairs a little advanced in front, and to the right of their respective tribes.'

To return to the main strand of this narrative: after the smallpox epidemic, it appears that from different parts of the Harbour area, the survivors regrouped to operate in the Middle Harbour-Manly area, which was about as far from the settlement at Port Jackson as one could get in the sheltered Harbour area while remaining on the coast. In addition, Middle Harbour was a rugged inlet that offered protection from the inroads of the colonists because it was difficult to approach from both land and water.

Were most of the survivors impinging on territory that was demarcated for another group? Were they refugees who streamed across a border, to be accommodated (whether willingly or not) by the inhabitants? One reading can suggest that this is what happened – if one accepts the existence of a 'tribe' called 'Cameragal' (Phillip's 'Cammeraygal'). If that is accepted, then the Middle Harbour-Manly area was part of traditional Cameragal country. Evidence to support this reading of the situation can be found in Tench, who wrote that the Cameragal had probably 'suffered less from the ravages of the smallpox'. Also, according to Collins, the Cameragal clan was acknowledged as being first among equals (my words) in respect of some rituals and customs. Collins said that 'their superiority partakes something of the nature of a constituted authority'. Further, describing the initiation ceremony at which a tooth was removed from young male participants, Collins noted that the ceremony could only be performed by certain men of the 'Cammerray' tribe. With these distinctions allied to its location, the tribe could have been the focal point for realignment and recovery after the epidemic.

If, indeed, the remnants of various clans came together in the traditional country of one clan, it would have caused tensions. Firstly, the amalgamation would have been haphazard and exigent, not orderly and considered, as was usually the case when Indigenous groups gathered. Secondly, it was happening at a time of huge psychic and cultural pressure, because phenomena such as the colonial invasion and the smallpox epidemic, neither of which had been experienced during thousands of years of Indigenous history, would have seemed cosmically inexplicable and relentlessly malign. Thirdly, with the remnants of clans amalgamating, the procedures for coexistence would have to be renegotiated.

However, there is doubt that a tribe or clan named Cameragal ever existed. For instance, Powell and Hesline stated that they were a 'hierarchical group but not a "tribe"' with significant functions, especially regarding initiation. Further, they explained that they were 'like the ancient rabbis, both ritual leaders and warriors'.

Whatever the case, whether the Cameragal existed as a separate entity and whether they occupied a separate territory, it looks as if the survivors of the smallpox epidemic came together to form a new group. There would have been jockeying and contending for leadership, with newcomers competing with existing leaders, and with competition among the newcomers themselves. Generally, male elders were leaders in matters of law and tradition, while younger, more vigorous men were leaders in other areas. Notably, younger men with leadership qualities, such as Bennelong and Colbee, were members of the new group. Perhaps the inter-group tensions, together with the need to live together, account for the fact that, as Hunter wrote about Bennelong,

> indeed, from the first day he was able to make himself understood, he was desirous to have all the tribe of Cammeragal killed, yet he was along with that tribe when Governor Phillip was wounded…

The following incidents and accounts suggest that by November 1789, Bennelong and Colbee were contenders for leadership positions, or already were leaders, in the new polity. Firstly, the boat party seized Bennelong and Colbee at Manly – those two and no one else – because they advanced ahead of the others. Secondly, when the boat returned with its prisoners, Nanbarry, the Indigenous boy who lived in the settlement, recognised and welcomed them, prompting Bradley to write, 'Colbey we have frequently heard spoken of by the Boy as a great Warrior and a leading Man among them…' Newton Fowell also reported their prominent positions, writing, 'On their Landing in Sydney Cove, Nanberry called them both by their Names, and he gave us to understand they were two Cheifs [sic].' Thirdly, Nagle, who was an eyewitness to the capture, wrote that Bennelong and Colbee were the 'head Warriers' and 'chiefs'. Fourthly, Hunter wrote that the two men 'appeard to have some influence amongst their Country men'. Finally, in a dispatch to Lord Sydney dated 12 February 1790, Phillip singled out Colbee as 'a chief, who had been frequently mentioned to us as a great warrior'.

The colonial records show that although Bennelong vigorously resisted captivity, he quickly adapted to his new circumstances and saw the possibilities that were offered from closer involvement with the settlement. Making a virtue of a necessity, he saw that his situation offered possibilities for him, as someone who was consolidating his position as a leader, and for his people. As Tench observed, Bennelong 'perhaps felt satisfaction in his new state'.

Bennelong had the intelligence, quickness of mind and adaptability to see the possibilities in his new situation. Tench wrote,

> His powers of mind were certainly far above mediocrity. He acquired knowledge, both of our manners and language, faster than his predecessor [Arabanoo] had done.

Hunter described Bennelong as 'a very intelligent man' who was also 'very good-natured, being seldom angry at any jokes that may be passed upon him'. Also, Tench wrote that Bennelong, 'though haughty, knew how to temporize. He quickly threw off all reserve…' Bennelong seemed to be instinctively open to absorbing and imitating the manners and customs of his new environment. For instance, Hunter noted that Bennelong 'readily imitates all the actions and gestures of every person in the governor's family'. Also, Bennelong quickly learned the table manners of English gentlemen; Hunter recorded that 'he performs every action of bowing, drinking healths, returning thanks, etc. with the most scrupulous attention'.

Bennelong soon acquired a hearty taste for European food and drink. Tench wrote, 'he became at once fond of our viands, and would drink the strongest liquors, not simply without reluctance, but with eager marks of delight and enjoyment'. It was a taste that, once acquired, stayed with him.

Bennelong was adept at grandstanding, which he did with relish. Tench recorded that when he asked Bennelong how he got a wound on the back of his hand, Bennelong replied that he got it while he was 'carrying off a lady of another tribe by force'. He added, 'I was dragging her away. She cried aloud, and stuck her teeth in me.' When Tench asked him what happened next, Bennelong replied, 'I knocked her down, and beat her till she was insensible, and covered with blood.' This might have happened – we don't know. However, in view of what we know about Bennelong, it was possible that he was playing the 'savage' to his gentleman audience, knowing that they pretended to deplore rough treatment of women even while they were titillated by tales of nubile, struggling females being dragged away to be ravished by lustful, virile males.

Another case of Bennelong's grandstanding was noted by Tench, who said that whenever Bennelong recounted his battles, he 'poised his lance, and showed how fields were won'. At the same time,

> the most violent exclamations of rage and vengeance against his competitors in arms, those of the tribe called Cameeragal in particular, would burst from him. And he never failed at such times to solicit the governor to accompany him, with a body of soldiers, in order that he might exterminate this hated name.

Tench's statement that Bennelong denounced 'the tribe called Cameeragal' and called down destruction on them, raises questions. Does this show that there was a clan called Cameragal? Or was this another misunderstanding, where a British observer was unable to separate 'political' division – that is, a clan or tribe, from 'functional' authority? Whatever the case, why did Bennelong want to exterminate 'the tribe called Cameeragal'?

Perhaps Bennelong wanted Phillip to mount an expedition so that Bennelong could, in the end, intervene and by so doing display his power and influence. In any case, Phillip would not launch an expedition against them, presuming that they could be identified as a separate group. Phillip wanted to subdue and 'civilise' the Indigenous people, not antagonise and eliminate them – and Bennelong would have known that.

We don't know whether Bennelong really did denounce 'the tribe called Cameeragal' and, if so, whether he used the term tribe, or some other designation. Nor do we know why Bennelong said that he wanted to destroy them – if he did say that.

Phillip honoured Bennelong in exceptional ways. Collins said that the governor 'treated [Bennelong] with every indulgence' and that Bennelong 'enjoyed every comfort which it was in his excellency's power to give him'. Tench wrote that Bennelong '[sat] at table with the governor' and called the governor 'beanga' or 'father', while the governor reciprocated by calling him 'dooroow' or 'son'. Also, Hunter wrote, '[Bennelong] walks about constantly with the governor… His dress is a jacket, made of the coarsest red kersey, and a pair of trowsers; but on Sundays, he is drest in nankeen.' The governor made Bennelong wear the thick kersey cloth, said Hunter, 'so that he may be so sensible of the cold as not to be able to go without cloaths'. The governor was trying to accustom Bennelong to wearing clothes, because this was an essential component of the civilising mission.

Bennelong was very well cared for. Tench wrote that even though the colony was suffering 'desperate circumstances' from a scarcity of food, Bennelong was so well fed that 'the ration of a week was insufficient to have kept him for a day'. This was done, said Tench, so that the Indigenous people would not know that the colony was in a weakened condition. Also, it would impress on Bennelong that the colony commanded extraordinary resources.

It appears that Bennelong learned a lot more about the colonists' culture, expectations and intentions than they learned about Indigenous people. Among the things that Bennelong learned (apart from the fact that he liked wine, as well as various European foods!) were that the 'visitors' were there to stay; that the colony was an outpost of a powerful and well-organised country that had only just began expanding in New South Wales and 'New Holland'; that Indigenous sovereignty and self-determination were of no concern to the colonising power; and that the deal being offered was that Indigenous people could survive if they surrendered and were incorporated into the colony ('voluntary subjection'), adapting to requirements but retaining parts of their culture and identity. On the other hand, if they resisted, they would be brushed aside and marginalised, as was already happening.

Tench wrote of Bennelong that 'his temper seemed pliant, and his relish of our society so great, that hardly any one judged he would attempt to quit us…' However, during May 1790, Bennelong did quit the settlement. What impressions did he take with him and what did he discuss with his fellows during the next six months up until the time when, during October 1790, Indigenous people began to enter the settlement voluntarily?

By this time, Indigenous people in the Harbour area would have little reason to doubt that the colony was going to expand without end. The evidence could be seen clearly. For instance, in a dispatch to Lord Sydney dated 13 February 1790, Phillip wrote that the country from Rose Hill to the Nepean River 'is as fine land for tillage as most in England' and was therefore suitable for 'those settlers which may be sent out'. The settlers would be placed 'at some distance from each other, for the conveniency of water (from one to two and three miles)'. Phillip assured Lord Sydney that the settlers would have 'nothing to apprehend from the natives, who avoid those parts we most frequent, and always retire at the sight of two or three people who are armed'. (Phillip proved to be over-confident, as will be seen.) This was written while Bennelong was residing as a captive in the settlement. While Bennelong would not have known what was written in dispatches, in view of his close relationship with Phillip, he would have been well informed about plans to expand the colony's population and territory.

In a dispatch to Lord Grenville dated 17 June 1790, Phillip again urged that more settlers should be sent out because he regarded them as essential for producing the stable and reliable food supply that the colony needed. Of course, growing numbers of settlers would add to the ever-increasing demand for land, thus relentlessly marginalising more and more Indigenous people.

As if to reinforce the message, during June 1790, one month after Bennelong escaped, four transport ships arrived, bearing more than 1,000 convicts as well as soldiers and officers of the newly raised New South Wales Corps. In addition, a store ship docked with provisions. The Indigenous people would have noted all these arrivals. They were further proof, if it were needed, that the 'visitors' were there to stay.

Expansion proceeded apace. During July 1790, one month after Bennelong escaped, Collins wrote that at Rose Hill (Parramatta)

> There also the governor in the course of the month laid down the lines of a regular town. The principal street was marked out to extend one mile, commencing near the landing-place…

The main street of the new town was two hundred and five feet (sixty-three metres) wide, with huts sixty feet (eighteen metres) apart, 'and garden ground for each hut was allotted in the rear'. A house for the governor and a barracks were also to be built. However, this was only the beginning; Collins wrote that

> by beginning on so wide a scale the inhabitants of the town at some future day would possess their own accommodations and comforts more readily, each upon his own allotment…

By November 1790, over 500 people were based at Rose Hill. These included twenty-four carpenters, twenty-eight bricklayers, fifty-two brickmakers, and 326 labourers.

Reading the colonial records, it looks as if there was a lull in relations between local Indigenous people and the colonialists from the time of the smallpox outbreak, through the time that Bennelong was captured, until early September 1790. As Collins noted,

> Since the escape of Bennillong the native in May last, nothing had been heard of him, nor had any thing worthy of notice occurred among the other natives.

One exception to the stalemate is on record. Ralph Clark, second lieutenant of the Marines, wrote that on 15 February 1790, he

> went up the Harbour in my Boat and went into Lane Cove where I was Yesterday to See Dourrawan and Tirriwan the two Natives that I exchanged the hatchet with Yesterday for there two Spears.

The contact was not entirely untroubled: Clark records that his three companions, comprising one soldier and two convicts, were so apprehensive and nervous, that he told them to use their muskets if anything untoward occurred. Nevertheless, the encounter lasted for two hours, during which time Clark met two of the men's children, but not their wives. There were other encounters, as is seen in Clark's statement that 'the Governour has often asked me as the Natives Seemd not So much affraid of me as the[y] are of every body else to take one of them and bring them in'. Clark did not try to capture anyone, even though he thought that 'Yesterday and to day I might with great ease and without running any danger have taken these two men…' He did not kidnap them because

> it would be very Ungenerous to take them for after the[y] had place Such confidence in use that I could not think of doing it for if I had taken them both what would have become of there young children the[y] must have Starved.

Of all the scores of thousands of words that I have read in which colonial commentators described Indigenous people and relations with them, Clark's words most reflect common humanity and decency. Despite the expectations of his superior, the governor, Clark would not betray mutual trust by kidnapping the men. Nor would he separate them from their children – because, if he did, who would care for the children?

However, common humanity and decency are not compatible with colonial projects. Events moved quickly after early September 1790. On 7 September, a boat party approached Manly Cove where, wrote Tench, the following occurred:

On drawing near the shore, a dead whale, in the most disgusting state of putrefaction, was seen lying on the beach, and at least two hundred Indians surrounding it, broiling the flesh on different fires, and feasting on it with the most extravagant marks of greediness and rapture.

When called, Bennelong stepped forward and asked about Governor Phillip. When Bennelong heard that the governor happened to be just across the water at South Head, wrote Tench,

> he expressed great joy, and declared that he would immediately go in search of him, and if he found him not, would follow him to Sydney. 'Have you brought any hatchets with you?' cried he.

Tench wrote that Bennelong was 'willing to instruct his countrymen'; in other words, he used the encounter to show off his new knowledge and skills, as well as his new acquaintances, to his fellows. Also, he would have had the distinction of conversing in English, which none of his fellows would have understood. Bennelong was given a shirt, which he donned, and then, a razor not being available, he used a pair of scissors to trim his beard. At the same time, wrote Tench, there was an ongoing demand for hatchets, which were not available.

The boat was dispatched to let the governor know that Bennelong was asking about him. Before the boat left the cove, wrote Tench,

> the natives…crowded around her, and brought down, by way of present, three or four great junks of the whale, and put them on board of her, the largest of which, Baneelon expressly requested might be offered, in his name, to the governor.

Bennelong was keen to meet Phillip on home ground.

Tench described the first phase of the encounter as follows:

> …governor Phillip stepped out unarmed, and attended by one seaman only, and called for Baneelon, who appeared, but, notwithstanding his former eagerness, would not suffer the other to approach him for several minutes. Gradually, however, he warmed into friendship and frankness, and presently after Colbee came up.

They discoursed for some time, Baneelon expressing pleasure to see his old acquaintance, and inquiring by name for every person whom he could recollect at Sydney...

Phillip poured a glass of wine for Bennelong, who drank it 'with his former marks of relish and good humour' and toasted the king 'as he had been taught'. Once again, Bennelong showed off his new knowledge.

According to Tench, the encounter proceeded in friendly fashion for about half an hour until

> a native, with a spear in his hand, came forward, and stopped at the distance of between twenty and thirty yards from the place where the governor, Mr. Collins, Lieutenant Waterhouse, and a seaman stood... He appeared to be a man of middle age, short of stature, sturdy, and well set, seemingly a stranger, and but little acquainted with Baneelon and Colbee.

With little hesitation, the newcomer launched a spear, which pierced Phillip's right shoulder with great force. Tench described what followed:

> Instant confusion on both sides took place. Baneelon and Colbee disappeared and several spears were thrown from different quarters, though without effect. Our party retreated as fast as they could, calling to those who were left in the boat, to hasten up with firearms.

Phillip was hurried back to the settlement, where the spear was removed. Although the wound was severe, it was not life-threatening and he made a quick recovery.

Next day, a boat party reported that at Manly Cove they met a group of Indigenous people, who told them that 'the man who had wounded the governor belonged to a tribe residing at Broken Bay, and they seemed highly to condemn what he had done'. Bennelong and Colbee also 'pretended highly to disapprove the conduct of the man who had thrown the spear, vowing to execute vengeance upon him'.

Collins recorded that Bennelong said that he and Colbee 'had severely beaten Wille-me-ring; and added that his throwing the spear at the governor was entirely the effect of his fears, and done from the impulse of self-preservation'.

When the name of the spear-thrower was learned 'from two Indians', wrote Tench,

> These two people inquired kindly how his excellency did, and seemed pleased to hear that he was likely to recover. They said that they were inhabitants of Rose Hill, and expressed great dissatisfaction at the number of white men who had settled in their former territories. In consequence of which declaration, the detachment at that post was reinforced on the following day.

(It is ironic that a complaint by two Indigenous men about the occupation of their country only resulted in the guard on the occupied land being strengthened.)

Next day, responding to a signal on the north shore, a party went across the water from the settlement and found Bennelong and several others there. At another meeting later that day, the officers gave Bennelong wine, beef, and bread, which he consumed. Then, wrote Tench,

> Having finished his repast, he [Bennelong] made a motion to be shaved, and a barber being present, his request was complied with, to the great admiration of his countrymen, who laughed and exclaimed at the operation.

Tench stated that there was such a friendly atmosphere that 'we began to play and romp with them'. Then, before they parted, Bennelong asked that some articles that had been stolen should be restored to the owner. Next day, having restored some of the stolen goods, they searched for Bennelong and found him on shore with his wife, Barangaroo. Tench wrote that 'On first seeing the boat, they ran into the woods; but on being called by name, they came back, and consented to our landing.' Bennelong, who was given wine, enquired 'with solicitude' about the governor's state of health. Before they parted, Bennelong was invited to visit the settlement and was assured that he would be welcome there. However, he demurred, and said that the governor should visit him first. Although Phillip did this, Bennelong still hesitated.

Collins wrote, 'Bennillong…certainly had not any culpable share in the transaction [that is, the spearing].' He also noted that when Phillip met Bennelong, the latter

> repeated his assurances of his having, in conjunction with his friend Cole-be, severely beaten Wille-me-ring; and added that his throwing the spear at the governor was entirely the effect of his fears, and done from the impulse of self-preservation.

Did either party really believe the other? It did not matter because the proprietaries had been observed while goals had been attained. Bennelong and his people had payback, while the governor at last was on track to securing the 'willing subjection' of the Indigenous people.

Now the door to relations between the two parties opened. Tench wrote,

> The eager desire by which we were stimulated to carry our point of effecting an intercourse had appeared. Various parties accordingly set out to meet them, provided with different articles, which we thought would prove acceptable to them.

Trading commenced, about which Tench commented, 'It had long been our wish to establish a commerce of this sort.' As an addendum, Tench added the sobering reflection that 'It is a painful consideration, that every previous addition to the cabinet of the virtuosi, from this country, had wrung a tear from the plundered Indian.' In simple English, all the Indigenous artefacts in collectors' cabinets in Europe had been stolen.

At last, on 8 October 1790, Bennelong and three companions visited the settlement. This marked the end of hostilities between the settlers and the Indigenous people of the Harbour area. Tench commented, 'From this time our intercourse with the natives, though partially interrupted, was never broken off.' Also, he wrote that by

November 1790, 'During the intervals of duty, our greatest source of entertainment now lay in cultivating the acquaintance of our new friends, the natives.'

This is a good point to stand back and ask what happened and, more importantly, why. The focus of the colonial commentators was the fact that the Indigenous people of the Harbour area had given up their hostility and alienation. From the earliest days, before the First Fleet even set sail, it was the wish of the authorities in London, channelled through Phillip, that the Indigenous people should be brought into 'voluntary subjection'. Now this had happened, even if an 'alliance' had not been established, because it was not necessary to establish an alliance with people who had given up the struggle. Also, Phillip could probably argue that he had largely realised his aim that 'nothing less than the most absolute necessity should ever compel him to fire upon them'. However, not everything had gone to plan. In view of the fact that the Indigenous people had suffered huge losses in land and resources, had lost at least half of their population to disease, and had suffered massive personal and cultural dislocations, all within the short space of two years, it cannot be argued that they had been treated with 'kindness', let alone with 'the utmost kindness', as Phillip wanted.

The colonial commentators recognised that the 'voluntary subjection' of the Indigenous people had come about because of one event, namely the spearing of the governor. Tench expressed this view when he wrote,

> That the foundation of what neither entreaty, munificence, or humanity, could induce, should be laid by a deed, which threatened to accumulate scenes of bloodshed and horror was a consequence which neither speculation could predict, or hope expect to see accomplished.

In short, it was a mystery – with a very welcome, if unexpected, outcome – why the spearing of the governor should have resulted in the subjection of the Indigenous people. How strange, indeed, when 'entreaty, munificence, or humanity' had not succeeded!

Collins called the spearing

a circumstance which seemed at first to threaten the colony with a loss that must have been for some time severely felt; but which was succeeded by an opening of that amicable intercourse with these people which the governor had always laboured to establish.

Significantly, none of the commentators tried to analyse what really happened. The goal of 'willing subjection', including some 'amity', had been attained. Mission accomplished. It was time to be grateful, and to move on.

But what really happened, and why? Let's start at November 1789, when Bennelong was captured. At that time, the Indigenous people of the Harbour area were in a distressed condition. Within the space of a few months, about half of them had died from a disease that had never been experienced, and that must have seemed like a supernatural visitation. At the same time, large portions of their territory, including resources on land and sea, had been taken by a superior force that had appeared out of nowhere, and that showed no signs of leaving or stopping its expansion. The reductions in numbers, the shrinking of 'country', and the decline in resources, had upset the structure and organisation of clan life and tribal relations. For survival, and to rebuild their individual and communal lives, the remnants of the clans had gathered in the North Harbour-Manly area, which might have been the traditional country of the Cameragal clan – if such a clan existed.

The 'rebuilding' process would have been stressful. There would have been jockeying for leadership positions in the new polity. Bennelong would have been one of the aspiring leaders.

Faced with distress, deprivation and new realities, there would have been intense discussions about how to proceed. It would have boiled down to three possibilities: (1) resistance to the invaders; (2) consolidation of the current position; (3) conceding to the invaders.

Then the settlers captured Bennelong. During his time in the settlement, he would have learned that the colonialists were even more powerful and potentially more numerous than was apparent. Also, he would have learned that they were not only there to stay, but that they intended to expand their territory and influence indefinitely, using their superior weaponry and technology, together with their much greater and ever-increasing numbers, as well as the efficiency of their centralised administration together with the back-up and support from their home base. There would be no let-up in the occupation of land and the appropriation of resources. Furthermore, he would have learned that the newcomers possessed resources that would be useful to his impoverished and harassed people (even if the colony was suffering from a shortage of food at the time). The colonists knew how to grow food, they had domestic animals, they had useful tools and materials, and they had access to seemingly inexhaustible (if sporadic) supplies of food and materials from overseas.

These would have been some of the impressions that Bennelong took back to his people during May 1790. In the light of subsequent developments, it is also likely that he counselled that the paths of resistance or consolidation did not offer good prospects. But if there was to be concession to the colonialists, how would it be done? Bennelong was the one person who could advise in the matter. He could lead the initiative and, by so doing, boost his stature as a leader.

However, there was one outstanding issue, namely payback (for which read 'restitution' or 'revenge'). Bennelong and Colbee had been insulted and humiliated by being manhandled and kidnapped, in full view of their fellows. Then, to add further insult and offence, they had been detained – in Bennelong's case, for more than six months. Bennelong could not hold his head high if he had relations with his captors without exacting payback.

But how was payback to be accomplished? How could Phillip be reached, when he was seldom in an exposed and unprotected position? To go into the settlement to accomplish payback would be suicidal – and, in any case, there would be a very low chance of success.

Then, at Manly Cove on 7 September 1790, there was a golden opportunity for payback when Phillip put himself in an exposed position, unarmed and not even backed up directly by muskets. (In fact, only two of the available muskets were serviceable, and they were left in the boat, on standby.) Not surprisingly, when Bennelong heard that the governor was nearby, he 'expressed great joy and declared that he would immediately go in search of him, and if he found him not, would follow him to Sydney', according to Tench. Also, Bennelong sent a large hunk of whale meat with the boat that fetched Phillip and 'expressly requested (it) might be offered, in his name, to the governor'. Bennelong was eager to ensure that the governor came to him, under conditions that he (Bennelong) could prepare and control.

Bradley, who based his account of the proceedings on the report of an eyewitness, Lieutenant Waterhouse, wrote that on arrival, after greeting, Phillip followed Bennelong and others into the bushes, where they conferred. After a while, Phillip went to the boat and, assisted by a sailor, fetched 'some Wine, Beef and Bread and some presents' and took them back to the group. Then Phillip returned to the boat and told Captain Collins that Bennelong and Colbee had absented themselves. He asked Collins to accompany him back to the group after which, said Waterhouse, 'as they went up I frequently heard a man on the right of them call out Benallon and told him of something he had observed'.

Bradley wrote that Bennelong was carrying 'a remarkable good spear' which the governor asked for as a gift. However, 'Benallon either could not or would not understand him but took the Spear and laid it down in the Grass.' This spear was used against Phillip.

The governor then asked Waterhouse to join them, after which the following occurred:

> The Natives appear'd now to be closing round us, of which the Governor took notice and said he thought we had better retreat, there were then 19 arm'd Men near us and many more that we could not see; The Governor then assur'd Benallon he would return in two days and bring with him the Clothes he used to wear and 2 Hatchets (which they are remarkably fond of) one for Colbey and one for himself with which they seem'd much pleas'd…

Bennelong delayed their departure for a few minutes by introducing some members of his group, including the spear-thrower who, when Phillip advanced to greet him, 'seem'd frighten'd, & seiz'd the Spear that Benallon had laid down in the Grass & immediately threw it with great violence, all those who were near retreat'd with great precipitation…'

Tench added the detail that the spear-thrower was 'seemingly a stranger, and but little acquainted with Baneelon and Colbee', while Collins stated that Bennelong 'presented to him [Phillip] several natives by name, pointed out one, whom the governor, thinking to take particular notice of, stepped forward to meet, holding out both his hands toward him'. He continued that the man might have thought that Phillip intended to take him prisoner. He picked up a spear from the grass and 'in an instant darted it at the governor'.

Although Tench and Collins thought that the spear-thrower acted alone, Bradley did not agree. He wrote, 'There are different opinions as to Colbey and Benallon being accessary to this assault, which I cannot but mistrust was the case…'

Significantly, when the governor first arrived at Manly Cove, there were times when Bennelong and Colbee absented themselves from his company. During this time, now that the governor had been delivered into their hands so quickly and so unexpectedly, they would have been arranging for payback to be accomplished. Was it significant that the agent of payback was an 'outsider' from Broken Bay? Was he really an outsider, or was it just a story that was made up to protect him? We don't know. However, we do know that a semicircle of men gathered as witnesses, and that Bennelong's spear ('a remarkable good spear': not just any spear, and not just anyone's spear) was used for the action.

All observers agree that the spear-thrower was standing close to Phillip, who even closed the gap between them by advancing to greet him. In view of this, and the fact that Indigenous men could hit targets very accurately over much greater distances, it is reasonable to infer that the spear hit Phillip exactly where the thrower intended – that is, in a non-vital part of the body. The intention was to punish him, not kill him.

Several aspects are puzzling about this payback incident. Usually the accused party participated in a ritual in which he could defend himself. For instance, this is seen in a description of a ritual that was printed in the *Sydney Gazette* of 17 March 1805 where a man named 'Goguey' was accused of murder. By dodging and using his shield, he was able to evade injury for a while until the following occurred:

> …three at once advancing upon him until within ten or twelve feet, he caught the first thrown on his target, but the second, discharged by Bennelong, entered above the hip, and passed through the side, so as to be afterwards extracted; but the third thrown by Nanbery as he wheeled to defend himself from the former, entered the back below the loins; when perceiving that his seconds had left him, he in a transport of rage and anguish turned his resentment upon those from whom he expected assistance but had deceived him, and then exhausted, fell.

The *Sydney Gazette* of 14 July 1805 also recorded an instance of one-on-one combat, where Bennelong and Colbee clashed over a woman: 'but half-a-dozen spears flying responsively without effect, their numerous seconds interposed, and here ended the affray'.

The point is that in traditional payback, the accused was forewarned and could defend himself. Also, it was an established ritual, in which the accused had seconds to support him. None of these conditions seemed to apply when Phillip was speared. However, the evident anxiety and nervousness of the spear-thrower, Willemering, could partly be attributed to the fact that Phillip was advancing on him without trying to defend himself, in violation of traditional payback behaviour.

But had Phillip been told that this was a payback ritual and if so, did he understand the implications? We don't know.

How do we account for the fact that Bennelong, Colbee and others distanced themselves from the assault on the governor, deplored it and enquired solicitously about Phillip's welfare? Well, they would, wouldn't they – if they intended to initiate improved relations with the colony? Phillip and his officers would not have welcomed improved relations if the prime mover of rapprochement, namely Bennelong, was identified as being the person who authorised the spearing. Nor would they have welcomed improved relations if the Indigenous people showed satisfaction at what had happened.

Bennelong's status as a leader was enhanced. But what was his goal as a leader? It could be said that he led his group toward release from an unrelenting, ever-tightening pressure. With Bennelong showing the way, the Indigenous people of the Harbour region gave up the unequal and debilitating struggle and, in return, received sustenance and personal security. The price was high: it included complete surrender of country and resources (most of which had been taken, anyway), together with surrender of autonomy, and amelioration of significant aspects of culture. As Achebe showed in *Things Fall Apart*, the Europeans brought improved material welfare – or, at least, access to more goods and technology. However, as an elder lamented in the novel, there was a big price to pay: the colonial administration, he said, 'has put a knife on the things that held us together and we have fallen apart.'

The last lines of David Rubadari's poem 'Stanley Meets Mutasa' resonate with this situation:

> The tall black king steps forward, / He towers over the thin bearded white man, / Then grabbing his lean white hand / Manages to whisper / 'Mtu Mweupe Karibu' / white man you are welcome. / The gate of polished reed closes behind them / And the West is let in.

In the case of the Indigenous people of the Harbour area, the opposite happened, with the same result: they entered the settlement, and so the West was let in.

Six
Children of ignorance

Although the colonial commentators recognised that the spearing of Phillip initiated a sea change in the relationship between the Indigenous people and the colony, they were not curious about why it happened. No one on record asked, 'Why did it happen? Why did it initiate a major change in the relationship?' They celebrated the fact that, at last, a breakthrough had been achieved, and that was all that interested them. In fact, across the years, one can still hear the collective sigh of relief that, at last, the deed had been accomplished. For instance, as stated above, Collins was happy 'that amicable intercourse with these [Indigenous] people which the governor had always laboured to establish' had been attained, while Tench enthused that 'The eager desire by which we were stimulated to carry our point of effecting an intercourse had appeared.'

Why (in their writings, anyway) were they so incurious about how and why something so momentous had occurred? Even if they did not know about payback, they did know that the change of attitude had to do with the spearing of a specific person, namely the governor. Why him, and no one else? If it was simple aggression, then why was only one person targeted when there was such a big imbalance in numbers, and the Europeans had only a few muskets?

One reason for the commentators' silence must have been that if they admitted that payback was the motive, then they would have to admit that a wrong had been committed, at least in the understanding of the Indigenous people. It would acknowledge what the commentators skirted around and avoided admitting, namely, that the Indigenous people had strong feelings, and a different point of view, about the colonial project. Also, they would have to admit that the rapprochement had been achieved through the application of Indigenous law and practice, not through British law and initiative.

Collins provided an unconvincing reason for lack of retaliation, namely that Phillip 'had always wished that none of their blood might ever be shed; and in his own case, when wounded by Wille-me-ring, as he could not punish him on the spot, he gave up all thoughts of doing it in future'. This is rationalisation: the real reason could not be stated, but something had to be said, so a convincing-sounding story was put out.

Another, more mundane, reason might be that the relationship with the Indigenous people was not always a priority concern for the governor, officials and officers. For instance, analysis of a sample of dispatches from Phillip to his superiors in London, three written during February 1790 and one during April 1790, shows that he was concerned with a wide variety of matters, as follows.

The first dispatch dated 12 February 1790 to Lord Sydney concerned

- increasing theft in the settlement;
- appointment of a night watch and complaints by the commander of the Marines, Major Ross, about the activities of the watch;
- difficulties of administering justice.

The second dispatch dated 12 February 1790 to Under-Secretary Nepean dealt at length with the disruptive behaviour of Major Ross and set out the difficulties of working with him.

The third dispatch dated 13 February 1790 to Lord Sydney concerned

- expeditions to explore Broken Bay and the Hawkesbury River, with descriptions of the land;
- discovery of the Nepean River (actually, the upper reaches of the Hawkesbury River);

- plans to develop Rose Hill (Parramatta);
- observations on methods of allocating land to settlers;
- routes by which convicts could be transported across the sea, and matters regarding settling convicts at Norfolk Island;
- opinion that the 'natives' only killed convicts when provoked to do so;
- smallpox and the death of Arabanoo;
- the capture of Bennelong and Colbee;
- the distribution of 'tribes' in the vicinity of the settlement;
- some observations on Indigenous customs.

The fourth dispatch dated April 1790 to Lord Sydney concerned

- the dire shortage of food and measures to deal with the crisis;
- dispatch of more marines and convicts to Norfolk Island, where they should rely on the island's superior fertility to support themselves;
- matters concerning the loss of the ship 'Sirius' at Norfolk Island;
- further observations about the dire lack of food, and a report about dispatching a ship to Batavia to obtain provisions.

To repeat: the relationship with the Indigenous people was only one among many concerns. In any case, the governor and his colleagues did not want to understand, or accommodate to, the Indigenous people. They simply wanted to minimise or eliminate 'trouble'. They wanted surrender, not a negotiated arrangement.

However, there is evidence that Phillip knew very well that he had been the receiver of payback. During December 1790, Tench was ordered to lead a military expedition to punish an Indigenous group that was held to be responsible for the death of the gamekeeper, McIntire (see later). Tench recorded that Phillip said that until then, all aggressive actions by Indigenous people which had resulted in the death of seventeen settlers had been caused by them (Indigenous people) 'having received injury, or from misapprehension'. Then came the crucial admission, when Phillip told Tench, 'To the latter of these causes…I attribute my own wound.' In short, Phillip knew, and surely so did those within the circle of authority (as well as further afield), that he had been attacked because cause had been given. However, it was only admitted incidentally, during the conversation that Phillip had with Tench.

On 8 October 1790, Bennelong and three companions were welcomed to the settlement. Hunter described the event as follows:

> [they] were kindly received, went from House to House, and saw all their old acquaintance, they receiv'd many little presents and return'd to their familys. When they thought proper; this Confidential Visit from two men, who appeared to have some influence amongst their Country men, soon brought about a More general intercourse…

(This suggests that Colbee was a member of the visiting party.)

Tench wrote that 'such numbers flocked to view them that we were apprehensive the crowd of persons would alarm them, but they had left their fears behind, and marched on with boldness and unconcern'. It is significant that even though the settlement extended across country that had been owned and occupied by Indigenous people only two and a half years earlier, the Indigenous people had been pushed so far aside that they were curiosities when they appeared in the settlement.

At the governor's house,

> Baneelon expressed honest joy to see his old friend, and appeared pleased to find that he had recovered of his wound. The governor asked for Wileemarin [the person who speared him], and they said he was at Broken Bay.

Soon, wrote Hunter, Bennelong seemed to be at home, 'running from room to room with his companions, and introducing them to his old friends, the domestics, in the most familiar manner'. Also, Bennelong was delighted to explain the use of unfamiliar objects to his companions; Hunter wrote that Bennelong displayed his 'importance to his countrymen' on this occasion, by the welcome that he received and by his familiarity with the situation.

Next, wrote Hunter, the men's wives and families visited the settlement. Then so many other families followed that soon 'every Gents [Gentleman's] House was now become a resting or Sleeping place for some of them every Night...' The next stage of adaptation was that the Indigenous people began to regard the settlement as a source of food; Hunter wrote that when they were hungry, 'they had immediat recourse to our quarters where they generally got their Bellys filld'. Adapting rapidly, the Indigenous people began to enjoy eating bread, which, noted Hunter, 'when we came here first, they cou'd not bear to put in their Mouth.' Even the little children began to ask for food: 'to shew us that they were Hungry, [they would] draw in their Belly so as to make it appear Empty'.

Collins noted that by 19 October, he and the other colonists were 'amusing ourselves with these children of ignorance...' It was not a remark that a senior official like Collins would make if he thought that a momentous event was occurring. Rather it suggests that he considered it to be of little consequence.

Blackburn recorded that Indigenous people 'often Come on board our Ship – which they Call an Island and Are Very troublesome for Bread which they Are Extremely fond of'. He also wrote that a house was built

> for a chief called Bannelong...where his wife, children and relatives often come and stay a day or two, since when many more men women and children are come among us, and are sometimes quite familiar, at other times as shy.

Tench provided more details about the house, writing that 'to please [Bennelong], a brick house of twelve feet square was built for his use... a point of land fixed upon by himself.'.

Hunter noted that rapprochement proceeded apace:

> Bannelong, with his wife and two children...now lived in a hut built for them on the eastern point of the cove; they were frequently visited by many of the natives, some of whom daily came to the

barracks: all of them were very fond of bread, and they now found the advantage of coming amongst the settlers.

Tench commented that Bennelong 'warmly attached himself to our society' because he was 'elated by these marks of favour, and sensible that his importance with his countrymen arose in proportion to our patronage of him…' He also noted that Bennelong's command of English was often useful but complained that 'he had lately become a man of so much dignity and consequence, that it was not always easy to obtain his company'. Here, Tench confirmed that Bennelong's status as a leader had increased, undoubtedly because he was able facilitate his people's entry to the settlement, where he continued to enjoy marks of favour and act as a mediator and interpreter.

Hunter noted the newcomers made themselves so much at home that 'that they often have a dance amongst themselves at Night on the lower point of Sydney Cove, where a small House had been built by the Governor's order for their accommodation'. Rapprochement was enhanced when a dance was held at the request of leading figures in the colony. Hunter took pains to describe the elaborate decorations and ornaments, the music and the intricate moves. In a spirit of amity, some of the colonists joined in, trying to imitate 'one of the most Striking moves' which entailed 'placing their feet very wide apart, and by an extraordinary exertion of the Muscles of the thighs and legs, mov'd the Knees, in a trembling and very surprising manner'. However, it was too much for the inexperienced Europeans: the move was 'such as none of us could imitate'. The goodwill on all sides was shown by the fact that

> They [the dancers] frequently at the Conclusion of a dance wou'd apply to us for our opinions or rather for marks of our approbation of their performance, which we never faild to give due praise to, by often repeating the Word Boojery – which signifies good, or Boojery Caribberie for a good dance, those Signs of pleasure in us, seem'd to give great Satisfacton…

By March 1791, about five months after Bennelong and his companions entered the settlement, Hunter wrote that

> the Natives being now become very familiar and intimate with every person in the Settlement, many of them now take up their rest every night in some of the Govt. [Government] houses. Their very unprovokd attack upon the Governor and his party being now past over and almost forgot…

Tench described at length a curious incident. Bennelong 'came to the governor at his house, and told him that he was going to put to death a woman immediately, whom he had brought from Botany Bay'. Tench wrote that it looked as if Bennelong merely wanted to inform the governor of his intentions and expected nothing further. However,

> His Excellency was so struck with the fierce gestures, and wild demeanour of the other [Bennelong], who held in his hand one of our hatchets and frequently tried the sharpness of it, that he determined to accompany him, taking with him Mr. Collins and his orderly sergeant.

Bennelong continued 'to talk wildly and incoherently of what he would do…'

When they reached the house, Bennelong attacked a young woman 'and gave her two severe wounds on the head and one on the shoulder…' Although the Indigenous people present did not interfere, 'either awed by Baneelon's superiority or deeming it a common case', the Europeans restrained Bennelong. Soon, after more wild talk from Bennelong, the Indigenous people present started to look aggressive and Phillip called for reinforcements, which arrived in the form of an officer and some sailors armed with muskets. However, Bennelong was not intimidated 'and boldly demanded his prisoner, whose life, he told the governor, he was determined to sacrifice, and afterwards to cut off her head'. Bennelong said that his grievance arose from an incident during a battle, when the girl's father had wounded him and the girl had treated him roughly.

Phillip ordered that the girl should be taken to the hospital, accompanied by a young man who claimed to be her husband. When Bennelong threatened that he would attack her there, the governor warned him that he would be shot if he tried to gain entry.

When Bennelong's friends did try to enter the hospital, they were driven away by armed guards. Then, after two days, Bennelong went to the governor's house, but was refused entry. However, Phillip ordered that he should be taken to where the girl was confined in hospital, 'to try if feelings of compassion towards an enemy, could be exerted by an Indian warrior...' Although Bennelong spoke to the girl in a kindly way, his wife, Barangaroo, reviled her. Tench concluded, 'Here terminated this curious history, which I leave to the reader's speculation.'

Two aspects of this incident are noteworthy. First, Bennelong was demonstrating his importance and influence. There was no reason why he should have told Phillip that he intended to beat the young woman (if, in fact, he really intended to do so) unless it was because he knew that Phillip would be concerned and would intervene, thus showing that he was interested in Bennelong's actions. Bennelong beckoned, and the governor responded. Hunter commented that Bennelong's behaviour was 'the height of savage insolence, and would have been immediately punished in any other person, and the governor was very unwilling to destroy the confidence Bannelong had for some time placed in him...' Also, the incident showed that Bennelong understood the European mind, namely the 'gentlemanly' concern that women should be treated 'gently'.

The second noteworthy aspect is that when the young couple tried to leave the hospital soon after they were admitted, wrote Tench, 'When questioned where they proposed to find shelter, they said they would go to the Cameragal tribe, with whom they should be safe.' What was Bennelong's relationship with the Cameragal tribe? Why would the young people be safe from him there? During his captivity, Bennelong inveighed against the Cameragals, calling them his enemies. Now the young couple claimed that the Cameragal group would give them refuge from Bennelong. Both cases indicate that there was distance between Bennelong and the Cameragal tribe.

Again, this raises the question: what was Bennelong's relationship with 'the Cameragal? Who or what were the Cameragal?

Even the governor's precincts were open to the Indigenous people. For instance, Hunter wrote that

> Early in the morning of the 13th of November, sixteen of the natives visited the settlement, and some fish being distributed amongst them, they made a fire in the governor's yard, and sat down to breakfast in great good humour: those that were strangers, appeared highly delighted with the novelties that surrounded them.

More than anyone, Bennelong frequented the premises and exploited his favoured status. At one point, Hunter recorded that after another disagreement between Bennelong and Barangaroo, who had a stormy relationship,

> a reconciliation had taken place, and they both dined with the governor in great good humour. Every thing this couple wished for was given them, and they had both fish and baggaray; but after dinner was over, the lady wanted to return, and Bannelong said she would cry if she was not permitted to go; so that late in the afternoon, the governor was obliged to send the boat down with them.

Later, Phillip and Bennelong had a falling-out over a hatchet that Bennelong stole in a fit of pique, but soon they reconciled. Hunter reported, 'in consequence of this reconciliation, the number of visitors greatly increased, the governor's yard being their head quarters'. Hunter said that the yard 'was always open to the natives…' Later, during May 1791, Hunter wrote that the governor had to remonstrate with Bennelong after he and others tried to abduct a young woman from the governor's yard by climbing over the fence at night. Hunter's comment on the incident was

> It was probable, that the displeasure of Governor Phillip with Bannelong would have a better effect than any corporal punishment,

which might only lead him to revenge himself on some of those who frequently went into the woods unarmed; at the same time, orders were given for the centinels to fire on any of the natives who might be seen getting over the paling in the night, and the sleeping of the women in the yard when their husbands were not with them was discouraged.

Then, during August 1791, Bennelong told the governor that Barangaroo 'intended to do him the honour of being brought to bed in his house'. However, 'at length' Phillip was able to persuade him that it would be better if she delivered the baby at the hospital.

The familiar way in which Bennelong, Colebe and their compatriots treated the settlers, including their homes, their food and their possessions, suggested that the settlers, with Phillip as their head, had been 'adopted' into the clan structure. Although something like this must have been discussed between Phillip and Bennelong before rapprochement was initiated, it was likely that no one in the colony, including Phillip, realised what it really meant. Were there times when Phillip sighed inwardly and regretted that he had allowed himself to be called 'beanga' ('father')? He must have asked himself whether there could have been other ways of bringing the natives into 'voluntary subjection' or at least establishing with them 'a strict amity and alliance'?

It is likely that the question of whether to establish friendly relations with the colonists caused a rift in the Indigenous Harbour group, which had been newly constituted after the smallpox epidemic by survivors. It looks as if the rift widened when some people followed Bennelong into the settlement, while others refused to do so. Perhaps the group even split in two. Possibly, among those who did not follow Bennelong were those who still called themselves the Cameragal because they lived in traditional Cameragal country and included Cameragal survivors of the epidemic. Or were 'the Cameragal as defined by Powell and Hesline, namely 'a hierarchical group but not a "tribe"' with significant functions, especially regarding initiation, 'like the ancient rabbis, both ritual leaders and warriors'?

Whether or not there were internal differences over relations with the colonialists, it looks as if most of the Indigenous people of the Harbour area became more amenable toward the colonists. This can be seen from an incident during November 1790, when a boat was wrecked at Middle Head, which is across the water from, and close to, Manly. The local Indigenous people reported the incident to the colonial authorities, set up parts of the wreckage so that it would be easy to locate from the water, and helped to recover the seine net. Colbee assisted with the latter action. Collins commented about the incident, 'This appeared to be a striking instance of the good effect of the intercourse which had been opened with these people…'

We can imagine two extremes of attitudes toward the colony, namely that while some Indigenous people entered the settlement, and felt secure enough to go there often and to remain there for long periods, others still shunned the settlement. Many would have placed somewhere between these two extremes.

What did Bennelong feel about the rapprochement with the colony which spread over the very country from which he and his people had been driven away (if we accept Phillip's description of 'Wangal' territory as lying south of the Parramatta River, and remembering that Collins wrote that Bennelong claimed to 'own' Memel/Goat Island, which is close to Sydney Cove)? When he was kidnapped, Bennelong had returned to his traditional country as a prisoner of the colony. Now, six months later, he and others were being allowed to return as outsiders and guests, restricted to residing in a small corner of what had once been their extensive country, while subjected to foreign laws and customs. Unsurprisingly, like many of his fellows, Bennelong moved between the two worlds, both physically and culturally. Tench wrote this about Bennelong:

> Clothes had been given to him at various times, but he did not always condescend to wear them. One day he would appear in them, and the next day he was to be seen carrying them in a net slung around his neck.

Reflecting on the condition of the indigenous Khoi Khoi ('Hottentot') people in the Cape Colony, South Africa, during the early decades of the nineteenth century, Thompson wrote,

> Now the white men claim the entire property of the soil and have even deprived the original possessors of the privilege of living free upon roots and game. They are accounted an inferior race and born to servitude. They feel their degradation, but cannot escape from it…

Did the colonists in New South Wales think on these things? Did they think that it was ironic that the Indigenous people, the owners of the country for millennia, were now returning on sufferance after they had been evicted? Did they find it poignant? Did they sympathise? Did they even wonder what the traditional owners were thinking? There is no evidence that the colonists entertained any of these thoughts and feelings. As stated, their only recorded reactions were relief that the Indigenous people had abandoned their hostility, and a quickening of scientific-like interest in the manners, customs, and cultures of these 'children of ignorance', now that they could be examined at close quarters.

What was the nature of this new relationship between the Indigenous people and the colonists? As seen above, Hunter wrote that soon after the breakthrough, every gentleman's house became a resort for Indigenous people, as well as a source of food. Does that mean that every 'gentleman' housed and fed Indigenous people from his own resources? Surely, the 'gentlemen' must have been assisted with rations and facilities from the commissariat store. Secondly, for how long would the officers put up with their quarters being used to accommodate crowds of outsiders? Not for long, one senses. Soon, other arrangements must have been made to accommodate the newcomers while retaining their favour and goodwill.

It looks as if Indigenous people were still being fed by the colony at least five months after the breakthrough. Tench recorded that on 11 April 1791, he was a member of an expedition that set out from Rose Hill (Parramatta) to find out whether the Nepean and Hawkesbury

Rivers were linked. Two Indigenous men, Colbee and Boladeree, were members of the party. Tench explained that they

> were volunteers on the occasion, on being assured that we should not stay out many days and that we should carry plenty of provisions. Baneelon wished to go, but his wife would not permit it. Colbee on the other hand, would listen to no objections. He only stipulated (with great care and consideration) that, during his absence, his wife and child should remain at Sydney under our protection, and be supplied with provisions.

It is significant that the two Indigenous men wanted the assurance that the party would 'carry plenty of provisions'. They could easily have lived off the land, so it looks as if they were demanding that they should be treated the same while on expedition as they were when they resided in the settlement. Also, Colbee confidently demanded that his wife and family should be provided for while he was away.

Tench commented that although the Europeans found the going tough, the two Indigenous men handled the terrain easily. However, they were bored and impatient, and demanded to know when the expedition would end so that they could return to the settlement. '"At Rose Hill," said they, "are potatoes, cabbages, pumpkins, turnips, fish and wine; here are nothing but rocks and water."' Also, when they met Indigenous people along the way, they told them about 'the stores we [the settlers] possessed and, above all, of the good things which were to be found among us, enumerating potatoes, cabbages, turnips, pumpkins, and many other names…' It looks as if the Indigenous people had become accustomed to the variety of food that was available in the settlement, and expected to be provided with provisions. That was a significant part of their side of the 'rapprochement deal'.

Another aspect of the relationship is shown in Tench's complaint about what he termed Colbee's and Boladeree's 'laziness': he wrote,

> they refused to draw water or to cleave wood to make a fire; but as soon as it was kindled (having first well stuffed themselves), they lay down before it and fell asleep.

Clearly, the two men did not make the trip as servants; nor were they there as regular members of the colony with duties to perform. They had a different, but not inferior, status.

What did Bennelong and Colbee discuss with Phillip when they met at Manly, when the spearing took place? What did Bennelong and Phillip discuss just before Bennelong led a party of three others into the settlement, soon to be followed by an influx of his fellows? They must have discussed the spearing. As they did on other occasions, Bennelong and Colbee probably expressed their pleasure that Phillip had recovered from the assault, their disapproval of the incident, and their dislike of the person who had done the deed. On the other hand, did they, perhaps, come straight out and let Phillip know that the spearing was payback for their captivity and that, from their point of view, restitution had been made? If so, how did Phillip respond? Did he say something like, 'I understand how you feel and why it was done. Let's put it behind us and move on.' We don't know.

What was the deal? Phillip must have told Bennelong and Colbee that they and their people were welcome to enter the settlement, where they would be housed and fed. The quid pro quo was that the Indigenous people would abandon their hostility, and would have to accept the rules and arrangements that the colonisers imposed. They must have agreed to terms, or rapprochement would not have taken place.

What were the finer details of the deal? Did Phillip specify details, or did events move so quickly, and was he so relieved at the outcome, that he worked out solutions as the situation developed? For instance, Phillip must have said that Indigenous people who entered the settlement would be accommodated at the homes of the 'gentlemen' – or why would they have gone to those places, and not to others? Also, he must have said that the 'gentlemen' would feed their 'lodgers' as and when required. However, these could only be temporary measures. Although the house that was built for Bennelong would have provided accommodation for some, it would not have been enough for all the Indigenous people who moved into the settlement, whether on a permanent or itinerant basis. Other, more durable, accommodation arrangements would have to be made. Also, arrangements would have to be made for feeding the newcomers – probably they were added to the long list of those who received rations from the commissariat store.

In time, the Indigenous people would have been granted precincts where they could find accommodation and make social arrangements that were to their taste.

Soon after arrival in Sydney Cove, on 7 February 1788, enlarging on his instructions, Phillip wrote that he was 'determined, if possible, to bring even the native inhabitants of New South Wales into a voluntary subjection; or at least to establish with them a strict amity and alliance'. Further, he wrote that, 'induced by motives of humanity, it was his determination from his first landing, to treat them with the utmost kindness: and he was firmly resolved, that, whatever differences might arise, nothing less than the most absolute necessity should ever compel him to fire upon them.'

How did the 'arrangement' with the Harbour people measure up to Phillip's early intentions? Firstly, although the Indigenous people had subjected themselves to the colony, it could not be construed as 'voluntary', in the light of the pressures to which they had been subjected, such as loss of land, loss of resources, spatial disruptions, huge cultural and political disruption, the certainty of more of the same to follow, and a disastrous epidemic. Rather, it was coerced. Further, although a form of 'amity' had been established, in the sense of an absence of overt aggression, there was no 'alliance'. Had they been treated 'with the utmost kindness'? Kindness – when by process of naked imposition, the colony had occupied most of the land, and appropriated most of the resources, of the Indigenous people of the Harbour region?

At least Phillip could reflect that there had been little use of muskets.

So began the long 'absorption' of Indigenous people into European ways and culture. Always, it was an absorption that was based on unequal power relations and continual expansion by settlers into Indigenous lands. Also, never again would the 'deal' be as favourable (relatively speaking) as that which was granted to the Indigenous people of the Harbour region, namely that they were provided with accommodation and food, and could freely move in and out of the settlement, in return for abandoning aggression and alienation. In future, as settlers occupied more and more Indigenous lands, the end was always the same, namely that the Indigenous people would either be killed (if there was resistance – and sometimes even if there was not), and/or would be driven away to survive as best they could, and/or would become serfs. The deal with the Harbour people was one of its kind, never to be repeated.

However, that was in the future. In the meantime, like the colonial district commissioner in Achebe's *Things Fall Apart*, Philip could write a treatise about pacification, if he wished. He could title it *The Pacification of the Primitive Tribes of the Sydney Harbour Region*.

Seven
Six heads

The calm waters of rapprochement were disturbed when John McIntire (Macintyre) was dangerously wounded on 10 December 1790. McIntire/Macintyre was a convict who served as 'gamekeeper' to Governor Phillip and, as such, was one of the few convicts who was permitted to carry a musket. On 9 December 1790, McIntire was with a hunting party that went to Botany Bay. The men were resting in a hut when they saw two Indigenous men armed with spears creeping toward them. According to Tench, McIntire laid down his gun, stepped forward, and spoke to them in their own language. After a short encounter, one of the men speared McIntire. He was taken back to the settlement, gravely wounded, and died soon afterward.

Although there did not appear to be an immediate motive for the attack, Tench suspected that it was motivated by revenge. He noted that McIntire had sometimes killed Indigenous people 'in his excursions' and noted that many Indigenous people, including Bennelong, hated and feared McIntire.

According to Tench, the soldiers said that the assailant was 'a young man with a speck or blemish on his left eye' who had been 'newly shaved', which showed that he had recently been in the settlement. Tench reported that Colbee and several other Indigenous people in the settlement identified the assailant as Pimelwi (Pemulwuy), who lived at Botany Bay. Hunter's comment on the identification of the assailant is significant because it reveals how close were the ties and contacts among the groups who inhabited today's greater Sydney area; Hunter wrote,

It appeared rather extraordinary that the natives should immediately know the man who wounded the game-keeper, and his tribe; they said his name was Pemullaway, of the tribe of Bejigal; and both Colebe and Bannelong promised to bring him to the settlement; but the former...went off, as was supposed, to Botany Bay.

To further illustrate the closeness of the ties, Colbee's wife came from Botany Bay.

Next day when Phillip returned to Sydney from Parramatta, he issued a proclamation that stated,

> Several tribes of the natives still continuing to throw spears at any man they meet unarmed, by which several have been killed, or dangerously wounded, the governor, in order to deter the natives from such practices in future, has ordered out a party to search for the man who wounded the convict McEntire, in so dangerous a manner on Friday last, though no offence was offered on his part, in order to make a signal example of that tribe.

However, Phillip ordered that no unauthorised person should 'fire on any native except in his own defence; or to molest him in any shape, or to bring away any spears, or other articles which they may find belonging to those people'. Further, the order stated that although natives would be punished 'for their own bad conduct', they would be 'treated with kindness while they continue peaceable and quiet'.

Phillip ordered that a party consisting of 'two captains, two subalterns, and forty privates...with three days provisions' should set out early on the following day on a punitive expedition to Botany Bay. Tench, who commanded the expedition, was ordered to kill ten Indigenous people and capture two as prisoners, after which, noted Tench, 'we were to cut off and bring in the heads of the slain; for which purpose hatchets and bags would be furnished'. Further, Tench was instructed that no huts were to be burned, that women and children should not be injured, and that friendly overtures should not be made, or responded to, 'for that such conduct would be not only present treachery, but give them reason to distrust every future mark of peace and friendship on our part'.

Clearly, Tench was unhappy about his orders; he wrote that, 'his excellency informed me that he had pitched upon me to execute the foregoing command'. He could have written, why me?

Tench reported that Phillip gave the following reasons for adopting 'measures of such severity': (1) 'since our arrival in the country, no less than seventeen of our people had either been killed or wounded by the natives'; (2) the tribe called Bideegal were 'the principal aggressors'; (3) Phillip was determined 'to strike a decisive blow, in order, at once to convince them of our superiority and to infuse an universal terror, which might operate to prevent farther mischief'; (4) Phillip had concluded that although the natives 'did not fear death individually, yet that the relative weight and importance of the different tribes appeared to be the highest object of their estimation'; and (5) he had delayed meting out punishment because 'in every former instance of hostility, they had acted either from having received injury, or from misapprehension'. However, said Phillip, he was convinced that McIntire was attacked without provocation 'and the barbarity of their conduct admits of no extenuation'.

Phillip also said that he was annoyed that although 'Baneelon, Colbee, and the other natives who live among us' had said that they would 'bring in the aggressor', it was plain that they had no intention of doing so. The governor told Tench, 'Nay, so far from wishing even to describe faithfully the person of the man who has thrown the spear, they pretended that he has a distorted foot, which is a palpable falsehood.' Phillip said that he was resolved to execute any captives 'in the most public and exemplary manner, in the presence of as many of their countrymen as can be collected'; furthermore, he would repeat the exercise, if necessary.

Tench requested that the expedition should be allowed to capture six people instead of killing ten. Of the six, some might be 'set aside for retaliation' (that is, executed) and the others might be freed later, as a warning to all. Phillip agreed, adding that if six prisoners were taken, he would hang two, and exile the rest to Norfolk Island.

Predictably, the expedition was a failure. After blundering about for three days, the soldiers returned to the settlement with empty hands. Collins wrote,

> There was little probability that such a party would be able so unexpectedly to fall in with the people they were sent to punish, as to surprise them, without which chance, they might hunt them in the woods for ever... The very circumstance, however, of a party being armed and detached purposely to punish the man and his companions who wounded McIntire, was likely to have a good effect, as it was well known to several natives, who were at this time in the town of Sydney, that this was the intention with which they were sent out.

In other words, the expedition was primarily an expression of frustration and displeasure.

Tench's description of the first day's work could have provided a script for *Dad's Army*, and it is worth citing at length, if only for entertainment:

> At four o'clock on the morning of the 14th we marched. The detachment consisted, besides myself, of Captain Hill of the New South Wales Corps, Lieutenants Poulder and Dawes, of the marines, Mr. Worgan and Mr. Lowes, surgeons, three sergeants, three corporals, and forty private soldiers, provided with three days provisions, ropes to bind our prisoners with, and hatchets and bags to cut off and contain the heads of the slain.
>
> By nine o'clock, this terrific procession reached the peninsula at the head of Botany Bay, but after having walked in various directions until four o'clock in the afternoon, without seeing a native, they halted for the night. At daybreak next day, they set out again. However, 'by a mistake of our guides' (!), wrote Tench, within a few hours, they found themselves on a shore within sight of five Indigenous men who ran away, pursued by the soldiers. The outcome was predictable: 'a contest between heavy-armed Europeans, fettered by ligatures, and naked unencumbered Indians, was too unequal to last long. They darted into the wood and disappeared.'

Tench wrote that 'no hope of success remained'. They found a small settlement consisting of five huts. However, it was abandoned and 'three canoes, filled with Indians, were seen paddling over in the utmost hurry and trepidation, to the opposite shore, where universal alarm prevailed'. Soon, they found Colbee fishing on the shore. He greeted them in a calm and friendly manner and, upon enquiry, told them that Pimelwi had fled so far southward that, wrote Tench, he could only be reached by a newly provisioned expedition. It was plain that Colbee was not telling the truth because Tench added, 'Had we known the account to be true.' The pantomime continued!

Colbee said that he had only left Sydney the previous day, 14 December. Tench's account is also worth quoting at length:

> He [Colbee] had it seems visited the governor about noon, after having gained information from Nanbaree of our march, and for what purpose it was undertaken. This he did not scruple to tell to the governor; proclaiming at the same time, a resolution of going to Botany Bay, which his excellency endeavoured to dissuade him from by every argument he could devise: a blanket, a hatchet, a jacket, or aught else he would ask for, was offered to him in vain, if he would not go. At last it was determined to try to eat him down, by setting before him his favourite food, of which it was hoped he would feed so voraciously, as to render him incapable of executing his intention. A large dish of fish was accordingly set before him. But after devouring a light horseman [a type of fish], and at least five pounds of beef and bread, even until the sight of food became disgusting to him, he set out on his journey with such lightness and gaiety, as plainly shewed him to be a stranger to the horrors of indigestion.

It was clear that Phillip had used numerous means at his disposal, even of 'eating him down', to prevent Colbee from spreading news of the expedition to the Indigenous people of Botany Bay! Of course, he could have detained him by force… To dissuade him by 'eating him down' – Phillip was resourceful, if not successful, in this case.

Phillip published the General Order on 13 December, and the expedition set out on 14 December. During the intervening period, Nanbaree learned of the contents of the order. This would not have been difficult, as Nanbaree spoke English and was a member of surgeon John White's household. In any case, the General Order was a public notice, and the expedition was well publicised. Would Nanbaree have delayed telling Colbee about the order? Would Colbee have waited until the next day before he set out on the short journey to warn the people at Botany Bay? On the contrary, it was all part of the pantomime.

That night, the members of the expedition settled down to sleep 'after a day of severe fatigue'. However, they were assailed by 'swarms of mosquitoes and sandflies, which in the summer months bite and sting the traveller, without measure or intermission'. Next morning, they set out for home, which they reached 'after wading breast-high through two arms of the sea, as broad as the Thames at Westminster'.

Phillip affected displeasure and Tench wrote resignedly, 'Our first expedition having so totally failed, the governor resolved to try the fate of a second.' Once again, Tench was given command; even more unhappy at the prospect, he wrote that 'the 'painful pre-eminence again devolved on me'.

The second expedition was also completely unsuccessful. This, too, could have provided material for a *Dad's Army* episode. Tench described how, in the dark of night, he and others 'were immersed, nearly to the waist in mud, so thick and tenacious, that it was not without the most vigorous exertion of every muscle of the body, that the legs could be disengaged'. After more fruitless searching, during which they did not see anyone, they returned to Sydney. Tench wrote sourly that they

> had passed through the country which the discoverers of Botany Bay [Captain Cook and his companions] extol as 'some of the finest meadows in the world.' These meadows, instead of grass, are covered with high coarse rushes, growing in a rotten spongy bog, into which we were plunged knee-deep at every step.

What was it all about? Clearly, there was never a serious prospect of capturing or killing any Indigenous people. They were forewarned and, in any case, they were too bush-wise, and too fleet of foot, to be apprehended. It was all a pantomime, partly to wag a finger at those who assaulted Europeans, and partly so that Phillip could be seen to be doing something.

Why did Tench write about the expedition at such length? Was it to give vent to his frustration at having to participate in such a pantomime? Possibly. Was it so that readers of his book would know that, no matter what happened later, something (no matter how futile) had been done to improve the security of the settlement and to make it safe from savage incursions and aggression? Possibly.

However, it was not all farce and bluff. The colonists would strike back effectively when pushed too close to home. Tench wrote that 'if we could not retaliate on the murderer of M'Entire, we found no difficulty in punishing offences committed within our own observation'. In this case, two natives were detected 'in robbing a potato garden'. A party of soldiers pursued them and, after dark, overtook them sitting around a fire with some women. Tench reported, 'the ardour of the soldiers transported them so far that, instead of capturing the offenders, they fired in among them. The women were taken, but the two men escaped.'

Two days later, some Indigenous people reported that a man had died of a gunshot wound. A party of colonists that included the surgeon went to the place. Tench, who accompanied the party, used the opportunity to make extensive observations about Indigenous burial practices and attitudes toward death. He even speculated about whether Indigenous people reacted differently to deaths from different causes:

> But how far the difference of a natural death, and one effected by violence, may operate on their fears to induce superstition…I leave to be determined. Certain it is (as I shall insist upon more hereafter), that they believe the spirit of the dead not to be extinct with the body.

Tench noted that Bennelong 'took an odd method of revenging the death of his countryman'. Bennelong and some other men robbed fish from a boat, 'threatening the people, who were unarmed, that in case they resisted he would spear them'. When the governor remonstrated with him about his action, Bennelong did not excuse or explain the incident, but rather 'burst into fury and demanded who had killed Bangai'.

In other circumstances, for payback, it is likely the death would have been avenged with the injury or death of a colonist. However, Indigenous people had the sense to know that soldiers operated under orders of the governor, who would not tolerate a challenge to his authority. Nevertheless, something had to be done. It was significant that the instrument of payback was Bennelong who, of all Indigenous people, had the highest standing with Phillip. It was also significant that the unusual measure of theft of fish, not attack on a person, was chosen as retaliation.

Collins reported a case of more orthodox payback justice when, during June 1791, some convicts destroyed a canoe that belonged to a young man named Ballooderry: 'His rage at finding his canoe destroyed was inconceivable; and he threatened to take his own revenge, and in his own way, upon all white people.' Although culprits were punished, with one being hung for the offence, this did not satisfy Ballooderry; a few days later, when he met a lone colonist near Parramatta, 'he wounded him in two places with a spear'. As punishment, the governor banned Ballooderry from entering any of the colonial settlements. This had the unintended consequence that 'the other natives, his friends, being alarmed, Parramatta was seldom visited by any of them, and all commerce with them was destroyed'.

Both cases illustrate that whereas British justice was based on identifying individual offenders and punishing them accordingly, a main principle of Indigenous justice was that an injury to one was an injury to all and that, moreover, justice should be administered by the aggrieved person or by those who were close to him/her. As Blackburn noted, '…among these people who make retalliation [sic] an invariable rule, the smallest affront on either side is sufficient to bring on a general battle'.

Collins provided a concrete instance of the workings of Indigenous justice when he described an event that occurred within Sydney settlement during December 1793. A man was accused of attempted murder and 'was obliged to stand for two evenings exposed to the spears not only of the man whom he had wounded, but of several other natives'. He could defend himself with a shield. On the first day, he was unharmed, and on the second day, he allowed himself to be wounded. That this was a formalised ritual in the service of justice is shown by Collins's observation that

> friendship and alliance were known to subsist between several that were opposed to each other, who fought with all the ardour of the bitterest enemies, and who, though wounded, pronounced the party by whom they had been hurt to be good and brave, and their friends.

Of course, there was more at play than a simple disparity in understanding about 'justice' and how it was administered. To the governors, the issue was clear: this was British territory where British justice ruled, irrespective of who was involved. On the other hand, the Indigenous people neither understood British law, nor recognised its authority over them, except where they were constrained by to do so by superior force.

For a while, relations with Indigenous people were settled. They moved into, and out of, the settlement peacefully, they resided there, and there were few incidents of violence between settlers and Indigenous people in the Harbour region. However, the military expedition to Botany Bay did not allay Indigenous feelings of anger and frustration and it was not long before Indigenous people, with Pemulwuy at the fore, were making concerted and deadly attacks on settlers.

Before moving to this phase, I will look further at how Indigenous people were accommodated in, and accommodated to, the settlement. Did they integrate fully, did they live within its bounds but fully apart, or did they integrate partially while maintaining a separate identity?

While living as 'guests' within the settlement, Indigenous people were also beginning to learn about, and adapt to, European culture and pursuits as Phillip hoped would be the case. For instance, during June 1791, Collins noted that because of the 'familiar intercourse which now subsisted between us and the natives', several of them had begun to sell or barter fish at Parramatta, for which they were content 'to receive a small quantity of either bread or salt meat...' The officers at Parramatta fond this trade useful, 'and they encouraged the natives to visit them as often as they could bring them fish'.

More proof of adaptation is seen in the fact that Collins recorded that during 1792, some Indigenous people sold firewood in town or delivered water. Payment might be in the form of 'worn-out jacket or trousers, or blankets, or a piece of bread'. He wrote that they were especially fond of bread, 'importuning with as much earnestness and perseverance as if begging for bread had been their profession from their infancy...' (Yet Tench noted that during the first year of settlement, 'If bread be given to the Indians, they chew and spit it out again, seldom choosing to swallow it.')

Collins noted an unfortunate result of adaptation when he reported that 'The venereal disease also had got among them [Indigenous people]; but I fear our people have to answer for that.' In this regard, he wrote that

> Several girls, who were protected in the settlement, had not any objection to passing the night on board of ships, though some had learned shame enough (for shame was not naturally inherent in them) to conceal, on their landing, the spoils they had procured during their stay.

Tench recorded that during February 1791, a ship that sailed from Sydney to Norfolk Island with supplies and reinforcements also carried 'A little native boy named Bondel, who had long particularly attached himself to captain Hill' and went with him 'at his own earnest request'. Tench explained that Bondel was an orphan. When the ship returned to Sydney, having left Bondel behind on Norfolk Island with his guardian, several Indigenous people enquired about his whereabouts and welfare. Smugly, Tench reported that on being told that the place he was gone to afforded plenty of birds and other good fare, innumerable volunteers presented themselves to follow him, so great was their confidence in us and so little hold of them had the *amor patriae* [love of homeland].

Ironically, Tench overlooked the fact that hundreds of Europeans, such as officers, administrators, soldiers and sailors, Tench included, had self-exiled themselves for considerable periods to this isolated colony, without aspersions being cast upon their love for their homeland or without questions being asked about their patriotism. Tench's comment reflected a desire to view Indigenous people as tenuously attached to their 'country', the better to excuse the colonial seizure of territory, and the better to be reassured that Indigenous people felt alienation of 'country' and destruction of lifestyle less keenly than did 'civilised' Europeans.

Collins said exactly the opposite about Indigenous people and their attachment to country. When Phillip returned to England after completing his service as governor, he took with him two local people. By a ship that left England after Phillip and his entourage arrived, the colonists learned that Bennillong and Yemmerrawannie were well, 'but not sufficiently divested of the genuine, natural love for liberty and their native country, to prefer London with its pleasures and its abundance to the woods of New South Wales'. Collins reflected that in spite of all the disadvantages and shortcomings of New South Wales, which was not 'the seat of arts and arms; the residence of worth, beauty, truth, justice' and lacked 'all the virtues that adorn and dignify human nature; and [of] all the pleasures and enjoyments that render life valuable', Bennillong and Yemmerrawannie showed that 'love for our native country' can exist 'even in a land where wretchedness, want, and ignorance have laid their iron hands on the inhabitants, and marked with misery all their days and nights'. (Wretchedness, want, ignorance and misery: Collins had a dismal opinion of the colony and the country!)

In the opinion of the colonisers, were the Indigenous people attached to their country and their way of life, or were they not? Did they feel their loss or, as Tench posited, had it passed them by, 'so little hold of them had the *amor patriae*'? The answer was that, to the colonisers, the issue was irrelevant. It was never a matter of much concern or interest, except to warrant an occasional murmur of regret and a momentary reflection that, sadly, this was the way it had to be. The colony would continue to expand, land would continue to be appropriated, and Indigenous people would continue to be driven away, subjugated or killed. The only amelioration was that during the earlier years, as per their instructions, the governors tried to implement a policy of 'amity and kindness' toward the Indigenous people. This did not mean that traditional livelihoods, living space and culture should be allowed to continue unimpeded; it only meant trying to minimise conflict and physical injury as expansion and land alienation proceeded apace.

Tench threw light on relations between colonists and Indigenous people within the settlement when he wrote that during May 1791, after Indigenous people had complained about repeated thefts,

> A convict was at length taken in the fact of stealing fishing-tackle from Daringa, the wife of Colbee. The governor ordered that he should be severely flogged in the presence of as many natives as could be assembled, to whom the cause of punishment should be explained. Many of them, of both sexes, accordingly attended.

Tench wrote that, as with Arabanoo when he witnessed a flogging,

> There was not one of them [Indigenous people] that did not testify strong abhorrence of the punishment and equal sympathy with the sufferer. The women were particularly affected; Daringa shed tears, and Barangaroo, kindling into anger, snatched a stick and menaced the executioner.

Apart from illustrating differences in notions of justice and punishment between the two cultures, Tench's comments are noteworthy for at least two reasons: firstly, they suggest that it was possible to assemble a reasonably large number of Indigenous people relatively quickly, which shows that they were within the settlement or near at hand. Secondly, they show that Phillip, having reduced the Indigenous people of the Harbour area to submission, was insisting that all colonists, no matter what their status, should treat them with consideration.

Writing of the situation during April 1792, Collins said,

> The natives had not lately given us any interruption by acts of hostility. Several of their young people continued to reside among us, and the different houses in the town were frequently visited by their relations.

Testifying to the social interaction that was taking place between settlers and Indigenous people, a 'Sydney pidgin' (my term) was already developing; Collins wrote,

> they conversed with us in a mutilated and incorrect language formed entirely on our imperfect knowledge and improper application of their words.

Thomas Watling, a convict who landed in Sydney on 7 October 1792 but wrote his account later, probably during 1793, criticised the governors for their misguided liberality and toleration of Indigenous people. He wrote,

> Many of these savages are allowed, what is termed, a freeman's ratio of provision for their idleness. They are bedecked at times, with dress which they make away with the first opportunity, preferring the originality of naked nature; and they are treated with the most singular tenderness.

He contrasted the treatment of Indigenous people with the lot of convicts who were '…denied the common necessities of life! wrought to death under the oppressive heat of a burning sun; or barbarously afflicted with often little merited arbitrary punishment…' From what Watling wrote, during 1793 Indigenous people were still being fed and clothed from the commissariat, and moved into, around and out of the settlement at will.

While Watling was an unusual convict in terms of education and because his artistic ability soon won him favours from authority, his comments do provide a rare insight into how 'ordinary' Europeans, like soldiers and convicts, might have viewed rapprochement. Very likely, to most of them, authority's attempts at conciliation and 'kindness' would have seemed a waste of time, effort and resources that made their lives more difficult by imposing limitations and constraints on their conduct.

Watling's resentment echoed seaman Nagle's truculence (quoted earlier) about the fact that 'the govener would not Allow us Arms to defend our Selves for fear we Should kill sum of them in our Own defence' and the off-handed treatment of 'One of the Natives [who] we New him to be One of those that Robed us…' As seen, Nagle and his companions got revenge by fooling the stranger into setting alight cartridge powder in his hand, which amused them greatly. There was no 'amity and kindness' in the attitude of these ordinary seamen toward Indigenous people.

George Thompson, a free settler who arrived in Sydney at the same time as Watling, provided useful information about how Indigenous people were relating to the settlement. According to Thompson, Indigenous people freely and frequently entered, and resided in, the settlement. He wrote, 'If they were shy at the first settling in the colony, that is not the case now, for the people can scarcely keep them out of their houses in daytime.' However, noted Thompson, this did not mean that Indigenous people had exchanged their traditional lifestyle and culture in favour of European ways; rather, they moved between the two, both literally and figuratively. Thompson wrote,

> They cannot bear to be confined to a hut or tent. The Governor has built a very neat brick hut for one of the chiefs, but neither he nor his family will live in it; they will sometimes stay at the place for a day, then make a fire on the outside of it. In short, they prefer living in the woods and going naked to the best house or clothes in the colony.

Emphasising the peripatetic habits of the Indigenous people, as they literally moved between traditional life – or what remained of it – and European lifestyle and culture, Thompson added,

> There are many of them that visit Sydney every day for the sake of what they can get to eat, and at night they return to the woods. There are three or four of the chiefs who attend the Governor's house every day for their dinner and a glass of wine.

From the latter comment, about two years after rapprochement began, Phillip was still wooing leaders of the Indigenous community.

Further, Thompson noted that some Indigenous people had already adapted to European life by taking up employment. He wrote, 'Several of the officers have both boys and girls as servants…' However, he was not impressed with their job performance: '…they are so lazy that it is with difficulty you can persuade them to get themselves a drink of water. If you attempt to strike them, they will immediately set out for the woods, and stay four or five days.' Furthermore, they were also unreliable because 'whether offended or not' they would often 'strip off what clothes they may have on, and take a trip to the woods'.

Thompson also commented that Indigenous people were 'very treacherous and deceiving' and gave as an example that they would spear and rob any settler who was alone in 'the woods'. However, they would not accost two or three people in a group, particularly 'if they have a musket, at which they [Indigenous people] are much frightened; few people travel the woods without one'. As both Thompson's words and subsequent events showed, rapprochement only extended to the inhabitants of the immediate Harbour region. Beyond that, in all directions, matters were a lot more fluid.

It is noteworthy that Thompson did not question, or comment on, the rapprochement. Perhaps he understood the political and strategic background to the policy.

Thompson's impressions occupy a place between the rapprochement-committed official accounts, on the one hand, and on the other, the resentful views of the convict Watling, and the chauvinistic attitude of the seaman Nagle. It is possible that Thompson's views represented those of a considerable number of 'ordinary' colonists, who phlegmatically accepted rapprochement as the governor's will – and the governor was nearest to God – but did not have good opinions of the culture, characters and behaviours of Indigenous people.

A short time later, during 1793, a Spanish visitor, Alessandro Malaspina, wrote that 'the measures taken by the English for the civilisation of the Aborigines had been humane and prudent'. He continued by commenting,

> The Spanish officers had seen Aboriginal men and women admitted to the houses of the principal individuals of the colony, where they had been regaled at table with the other guests. Families of Aborigines had cheerfully greeted the Spaniards in English, and on occasion they had been observed singing and dancing the whole night long around campfires in the main streets of the settlement, without anyone molesting them (quoted in King, 1986).

David Collins summed up the situation during September 1796 when he wrote,

> ...that friendly intercourse with the natives which had been so earnestly desired was at length established; and having never been materially interrupted, these remote islanders have been shown living in considerable numbers among us without fear or restraint; acquiring our language; readily falling in with our manners and customs; enjoying the comforts of our clothing, and relishing the variety of our food...

Collins attested that official policy was permissive as long as the natives were not troublesome when he added,

> They have been always allowed so far to be their own masters, that we never, or but rarely, interrupted them in any of their designs, judging that by suffering them to live with us as they were accustomed to do before we came among them, we should sooner attain a knowledge of their manners and customs.

His reference to the fact that Indigenous people were 'enjoying' the use of European clothing and 'relishing' European food, suggests that they were still being provided with these articles by the commissariat.

Again, Collins referred to the development of a Sydney pidgin when he noted, 'they conversed with us in a mutilated and incorrect language formed entirely on our imperfect knowledge and improper application of their words'. He also termed it 'nothing but a barbarous mixture of English with the Port Jackson dialect'. The existence of the pidgin tells us a lot about the relationship between the settlers and the Indigenous people who frequented the settlement. Pidgins arise where two language groups have regular but functionally limited interactions and do not integrate socially. Furthermore, contrary to what Collins said, a pidgin develops when both parties adapt to find common communicative ground in the simplified 'language' that becomes the pidgin.

In summary, the development of the Sydney pidgin tells us that although the two societies had close contact with each other, the relationship stopped far short of integration; furthermore, it shows that communication between the two groups was mainly functional and transactional in nature. The existence of the pidgin also supports Collins's contention that 'They have been always allowed so far to be their own masters…' because it shows that at this point in relations, colonial domination had not extended to rigorous cultural suppression.

Collins' assertion that Indigenous people 'have been always allowed so far to be their own masters' also applied to law and justice, as long as affairs only involved Indigenous people. For instance, based on traditional law and practices, they could stage ceremonial fights, settle affairs of honour, and engage in payback. British law only intruded when a British citizen was involved, as when Phillip censured Bennelong and Ballooderry for exacting payback where Europeans were involved.

David Dickenson Mann, a convict who arrived in 1799, wrote that by 1796,

> The natives had been, of late years, perfectly reconciled to their new countrymen; and, although their attachment to their accustomed habits and situations induced them to abstain from taking up new residences, and from mixing indiscriminately with the Europeans, they had become comparatively social, and commenced

an intercourse which was calculated to rivet the prosperity of the colony.

As Mann was not an eyewitness, but rather was reporting what he was told, it is not certain that he was reliable. Nevertheless, it is interesting that he wrote that the natives had not '[taken] up new residences' but rather kept to themselves, even if they had become 'comparatively social'.

In time, Indigenous people resorted to the court to settle grievances against British citizens. For instance, on 23 February 1811, the *Sydney Gazette* reported a court case in which an Indigenous man claimed that he had not been properly remunerated for his work as a sailor during a voyage.

In February 1795, Collins noted that 'the natives adjusted some affairs of honour in a convenient spot near the brick-fields'. The brickfields, which were located between today's Town Hall and Central Station (thus only a short distance from Sydney Cove), seem to have become a place where Indigenous people congregated. It is interesting that Collins also mentions that 'the people who live about the south shore of Botany Bay' were numbered among the familiars of the settlement and that Indigenous people felt sufficiently 'at home' to host a trial-of-strength battle at which one of the champions was a stranger who 'had been several days on his journey from the place where he lived, which was far to the southward'.

Testifying to the degree of proximity between the two races, during late 1796, Collins noted,

> when they [Indigenous people] assembled to dance or to fight before our houses, we never dispersed, but freely attended their meetings. To them this attention of ours appeared to be agreeable and useful; for those who happened to be wounded in their contests instantly looked out for one of our surgeons...

By 1805, Indigenous people still frequented central parts of the settlement. For instance, the *Gazette* of 14 July 1805 reported that a ritual contest between Bennelong and Colbee took place at Farm Cove, which was adjacent to the centre of the settlement at Sydney Cove (as it was called: today it encompasses Circular Quay, the Rocks, and Bennelong Point). The newspaper reported that twice during December 1805, once for ritual combat and once for a funeral, Indigenous people assembled at the brickfields. During the following month, another ritual combat took place in front of the military barracks.

On 25 December 1808, the *Gazette* reported that Indigenous people engaged in 'a desperate fight, which was kept up for several hours' in front of 'the new Military Barrack', while on 15 January 1809, the newspaper reported that 'a number of natives collected at the back of the Dry Store, for the purpose of inflicting punishment'.

On 27 November 1813, the *Gazette* reported that 'A well known useful native, named Boggara, but commonly called Mendoza' had been buried at Woolloomooloo, which is less than two kilometres from Sydney Cove. The report also stated that 'The deceased was a native of Broken Bay, from whence a formidable party were in attendance to avenge his death, although by human hands he fell not.' This report suggests that twenty-three years after rapprochement began, Indigenous people were still frequenting central areas of the settlement, where they could conduct ceremonies unimpeded. The reference to 'a native of Broken Bay' and his compatriots also suggests that Indigenous people from relatively distant parts enjoyed free access to central areas of the settlement.

Rapprochement post-1790 between settlers and Indigenous people in the Harbour region has sometimes been celebrated as a brief period of peace and even inter-cultural bonding that marked a 'truce' in the attrition and aggression between settlers and Indigenous people. Sometimes it is portrayed rather like the soccer games, carol-singing, and fraternisation between enemies that stopped the fighting in parts of the Western Front for a short time during December 1914. However, while hostilities did cease, it must be remembered that rapprochement only came about because the Indigenous people had been reduced to dire straits by disease, land alienation and destruction of their resources, and because leaders such as Bennelong saw both personal and wider advantages in allying with, rather than being hostile to, the colony. It must also be remembered that rapprochement only affected the Indigenous people of the Harbour region – and probably not all of them, either. At most, only a few hundred Indigenous people were involved. As Hunter noted, at the time that rapprochement began,

> Bannelong and the girl who lived with the clergyman had repeatedly said, that the tribes which resided about Botany-Bay and the inland parts near the head of that harbour, always killed the white man.

Beyond the Harbour region, towards Botany Bay and southward, westward toward Parramatta and the Blue Mountains, north-westward toward the Hawkesbury, and to all points north of Sydney, there was no rapprochement. As the colony extended, so did hostilities which, sector by sector, only ended when all the Indigenous people had either been killed, had fled, or had been subjugated.

Robert J. King (1986) summed up the rapprochement situation when he wrote, 'After an initial period of intense hostility, the Eora had apparently come to terms with the futility of trying to resist the newcomers.' He stated that 'efforts by the English settlers to gain the goodwill of the Aborigines while occupying their lands' were 'well-intentioned but clumsy and even self-defeating' and went on to say that 'the Eora [were] powerless to prevent this "usurpation" of their rights (as Malaspina referred to the process of English colonization in his report) but unwilling and unable to give up their own way of life and become "civilized" as the Europeans wished. In the Sydney of the 1790s, English and Eora dwelt side by side, in a kind of uneasy peaceful coexistence.' (Malaspina was a Spanish explorer who visited the NSW settlement during 1793.)

Rapprochement was a complex and intense period in relations between Indigenous people and the colonisers. However, despite the amount of attention that it has attracted, it was a one-off occurrence, an anomaly rather than a trendsetter, that affected few Indigenous people and covered a limited amount of colonial space.

Eight
A state of war

John Hunter (September 1795–September 1800) and Philip Gidley King (September 1800–August 1806), were the second and third members of the three-member 'old guard' of governors. As First Fleeters who had worked closely with Phillip, they understood how and why 'rapprochement' had occurred and why it was useful. When commissioned, all three received the same royal orders regarding relations with the Indigenous people – namely, 'You are to endeavour by every possible means to extend your intercourse with the natives and to conciliate their affections, enjoining all our subjects to live in amity and kindness with them…' By trying to reconcile the unreconcilable, these three officers provided continuity in policy and approaches toward Indigenous people.

Writing to his successor, William Bligh, Governor King said of the Indigenous people,

> Much has been said about the propriety of their being compelled to work as Slaves, but as I have ever considered them the real Proprietors of the Soil, I have never suffered any restraint whatever on these lines, or suffered any injury to be done to their persons or property. (Quoted in Roe, 1958)

Philip Gidley King was the last governor to express the sentiment that Indigenous people were 'the real Proprietors of the Soil'. (However, events often contradicted his words.)

Rapprochement was not smooth sailing. It did produce stresses and strains. For instance, as seen above, Thompson (and no doubt other colonists) thought that Indigenous people were not only lazy and unreliable as employees but were also 'treacherous and deceiving'. Colonists thought that Indigenous people were idle and 'uncivilised' and resented the fact that they were given privileges such as living off the common store, especially as few of them did wage labour for a living. Another charge was made by Collins, who wrote during 1796, 'Those natives who lived with the settlers had tasted the sweets of a different mode of living' and either stole from those with whom they lived, or taught others to do so. Generally, colonists made little effort to understand Indigenous culture; nor was there much reciprocity, except as needs dictated: as a result, while there was coexistence, there was little appreciation or integration.

While relations within the Sydney settlement were relatively stable, relations in the outer districts were not only a lot less harmonious but were on a deteriorating course. The Hawkesbury quickly became a flashpoint, partly because the occupied area was fertile and well-watered. During March 1794, Collins wrote,

> From the settlement on the banks of that river [Hawkesbury] the best reports continued to be received from time to time: every where the settlers found a rich black mould of several feet depth, and one man had in three months planted and dug a crop of potatoes.

In the same vein, on 4 April 1794, Lieutenant-Governor Paterson wrote to Secretary of State Henry Dundas,

> I have settled on the banks of the Hawkesbury twenty-two settlers, who seem very much pleased with their farms. They describe the soil as particularly rich, and they inform me whatever they have planted has grown in the greatest luxuriance.

In a later dispatch to Dundas, dated 15 June 1795, Paterson described the Hawkesbury area as 'the most fertile spot which has yet been discovered in the colony'. He also wrote,

> The number of settlers on the banks of the Hawkesbury, with their families, amounts to upwards of four hundred persons, and their

grounds extend near thirty miles along the banks on both sides of the river.

At the same time, Collins wrote, 'in general their [the settlers'] grounds which had been in wheat had produced from thirty to thirty-six bushels an acre...'

Indigenous people were alarmed and provoked by this escalating intrusion on their land and resources. During May 1795, Collins wrote that at the Hawkesbury, 'an open war seemed about this time to have commenced between the natives and the settlers...' Two settlers had been killed and

> the natives appeared in large bodies, men, women, and children, provided with blankets and nets to carry off the corn... In their attacks they conducted themselves with much art; but where that failed they had recourse to force, and on the least appearance of resistance made use of their spears or clubs.

The colonial response was swift and determined: a military detachment was sent to the Hawkesbury,

> with instructions to destroy as many as they could meet with of the wood tribe (Be-dia-gal); and, in the hope of striking terror, to erect gibbets in different places, whereon the bodies of all they might kill were to be hung.

It was reported that several Indigenous people were killed, although their bodies were not found. Also, prisoners were taken to Sydney, comprising 'one man, (apparently a cripple,) five women, and some children'. One woman, 'with a child at her breast, had been shot through the shoulder, and the same shot had wounded the babe. They were immediately placed in a hut near our hospital, and every care taken of them that humanity suggested.' The man escaped, but the women were kept as hostages in the hope that 'by detaining the prisoners and treating them well, some good effect might result...' After a while they were released; however, during their period of detention, 'the wounded child died, and one of the women was delivered of a boy, which died immediately'. Shortly afterwards, when the military detachment withdrew, 'the natives attacked a farm nearly opposite Richmond Hill, belonging to one William Rowe, and put him and a very fine child to death…' Rowe's wife escaped with wounds. Almost certainly, this was a case of payback.

Collins wrote that that from now onwards, the military detachment would be permanently based at the Hawkesbury, 'and the soldiers were distributed among the settlers for their protection…' He added that it was 'a protection, however, that many of them did not merit'. The last comment, revealing suspicion and mistrust between authorities and settlers at the Hawkesbury, is significant in the light of later events. Did Collins make this sour observation because so many settlers were ex-convicts and therefore, in his opinion, not worthy of the time, expense and effort that was spent on protecting them? Or did Collins make this comment because he thought that the settlers were guilty of provoking the violence? It was probably mainly the latter, in the light of Collins's comment (October 1794) that

> whatever the settlers at the river suffered was entirely brought on them by their own misconduct…but nothing seemed to deter them [Indigenous people] from prosecuting the revenge they had vowed against the settlers for the injuries they had received at their hands.

Similarly, in a dispatch to the Duke of Portland dated 2 January 1800, Governor Hunter referred to 'this horrid practice of wantonly destroying the natives'. He continued, 'Much of that hostile disposition which has occasionally appeared in those [Indigenous] people has been but too often provoked by the treatment which many of them have received from the white inhabitants.' In the same dispatch, referring to the 'Hawkesbury trial' (see later), he wrote,

> You will discover, my Lord, what a host of evidence is brought forward from that quarter [that is, the accused settlers] to prove what numbers of white people have been kill'd by the natives; but cou'd we have brought with equal ease such proofs from the natives as

they are capable of affording of the wanton and barbarous manner in which many of them have been destroy'd…we shou'd have found an astonishing difference in the numbers.

In a dispatch dated 20 June 1797, Hunter wrote to the Duke of Portland that

> The worst characters have unfortunately been placed at the greatest distance from head-quarters (the banks of the Hawkesbury), where a considerable number of them refus'd lately to obey a Public Order I had occasion to issue, and did not hesitate to say that they did not care for the Governor or the Orders of the colony – they were free men, and wou'd do as they pleas'd. I, however, very soon convinc'd them of their mistake, and they became very humble, and promis'd the strictest obedience in future if I wou'd pardon this offence. This turbulent conduct cou'd never have happen'd had these people been kept under proper regulations from the beginning.

The governor did not trust the settlers, even as he was obliged to support them, and they did not trust him, even as they needed his support.

What did the authorities in Sydney expect would happen when they allocated Indigenous lands to settlers? Did they suppose that Indigenous people would just shrug, make way and accept the situation? Did they not anticipate that Indigenous people would fight to retain their land, and did they not suppose that the settlers would fight back? In a sense, the settlers, too, were 'victims' of the situation. The settlers recognised the state, in the person of the governor, as the only authority, and the state had granted them the land. That being the case, in their view, they had a right to the land, and they would defend themselves and their land if the state could not, or would not, do it.

In his dispatch of 15 June 1795 to Dundas, which adds some details to Collins's account, Paterson wrote,

> They [settlers] have for some time past been annoyed by the natives, who have assembled in large parties for the purpose of plundering

them of their corn; and from the impossibility of furnishing each settler with firearms for his defence, several accidents have happened. Within a few weeks five people have been killed and several wounded.

Paterson told Dundas that he had sent a detachment of the New South Wales Corps to the area, 'to drive the natives to a distance, as for the protection of the settlers'. On the night after the detachment's arrival, wrote Paterson,

> the party had fired upon and pursued a large body of natives, who had concealed themselves in the neighbouring woods during the day, and at night came to a settler's farm to plunder it...

The commander of the detachment reported that 'he supposes seven or eight natives were killed, and that he was taking every measure he thought likely to deter them from appearing there again'. Concerning hostages, Paterson wrote,

> I mean to keep them until they can be made to understand that it is not their interest to do us injuries, and that we are readier to be friends than enemies; but that we cannot suffer our people to be inhumanly butchered, and their labour rendered useless by their depredations, with impunity.

Paterson concluded by stating that he regretted being forced to 'destroy any of these people particularly as I have no doubt of their having been cruelly treated by some of the first settlers who went out there'. However, if he had not taken this step, 'every prospect of advantage which the colony may expect to derive from a settlement formed on the banks of so fine a river as the Hawkesbury would be at an end'. Once again, authority not only felt that it had been frustrated by the behaviour of the settlers, but also recognised that it could do little to favourably influence the situation, which now had its own momentum.

By early 1796, the governor proclaimed something like a 'state of emergency' at the Hawkesbury. The Government and General Order of 22 February 1796 addressed 'The frequent attacks and depredations to which the settlers situated on the banks of the Hawkesbury and other places are liable from the natives' and ordered all farmers and their families to assemble for mutual protection 'whenever any numerous body of the natives are known to be lurking about the farms'. Reflecting the usual ambivalence that emanated from authority when it came to violence between settlers and Indigenous people, the directive would have created confusion when it went on to state, 'it is his Excellency's positive injunction to the settlers and others who have firearms that they do not wantonly fire at or take the lives of any of the natives' on pain of being accused of assault or murder.

How were the settlers to decide whether natives were 'lurking', as opposed to visiting or passing by (which they often did), and how were they to decide the difference between 'wantonly' and justifiably firing at and/or killing natives? It was a desperate measure by the governor, reflecting his exasperation and frustration at a situation that was escalating out of control.

Relations continued to deteriorate, as can be seen from the proceedings of a court case four years later. The court convened in Sydney on 14 October 1799, to try five settlers for the murder of two young Indigenous men in the Hawkesbury region. The settlers all lived along the river, close to the site of the modern town of Windsor. The court heard that the two men were killed because they were believed to have been involved in the murder of two settlers, Hodgkinson and Wimbo, although there was no hard proof that this was the case.

The fraught nature of relations in the region is shown by the estimates that were made of deaths and injuries in inter-racial violence. Lieutenant Hobby, the commanding officer of the New South Wales Corps detachment at the Hawkesbury, testified that during the two months that he had held the command, two settlers had been killed, as well as 'one wounded so as to be left for dead, one attacked, and repeated Thefts'. Two natives had 'been killed by the White People'.

Robert Braithwaite, settler, testified that during the twelve months that he had resided at the Hawkesbury,

I recollect four men to have been killed and Goodall to have been very Desperately Wounded by them and that a servant of mine was attacked by several Natives one of whom he had shot in his own Defence after having been robbed of a Kangaroo he had killed.

He stated that 'about five' natives had been killed, 'including the one killed by my servant'.

David White, settler, testified that he had lived at the Hawkesbury for about five or six years, during which time, 'to the best of my Recollection Twelve White Persons have been put to Death by the Natives' while about twenty natives had been killed. John Francis Molloy, who was described as holding the position of acting surgeon 'in consequence of no regular Surgeon acting at the Hawkesbury', testified that 'in the course of his practice for four years and a half, Twenty Six White People have been killed by the Natives and 13 Wounded on the Banks of the Hawkesbury'. He said that 'several of them were killed and wounded in defending their property against the depredations of the Natives'.

Lieutenant Hobby was asked, 'What is the state of Security or Danger of the Settlers at the Hawkesbury with respect to the Natives?' He replied,

> I conceive the property of the Settlers on the Front Farms to be perfectly secure in popular situations – those of the back Farms and above the Creek in remote situations are exposed to great Danger from the Natives – I think the Persons of the People insecure both on the Farms and when they may be travelling on the roads – I have known several single Persons to have been attacked on the roads by the Natives altho' such Persons were armed.

By 'popular situations', Hobby almost certainly meant those that were more densely populated.

For an insight into how individuals felt about the security situation, we have the testimony of Isabella Ramsay, who was asked, 'Why did you stand so much in fear of the Natives – have you ever sustained any loss or injury by them?' She replied,

We have been robbed by the Natives, but from their general inhuman behaviour I was the more afraid of them – and from hearing of the many depredations they committed.

As always, the root cause of the violence and insecurity was the fact that the Indigenous people were resisting the theft of their land and resources, which were being appropriated at an ever-increasing rate. However, as is common in prolonged disputes, original causes are often submerged under the flood of more recent grievances. In this case, the mutual viciousness that accompanied the aggression exacerbated the conflict. For instance, Lieutenant Hobby testified that

> the hands of both the deceased boys were tied behind them, and that there was a wound through the body of the least of the boys, as if given by a Cutlass, and another wound on or about the hip as if given also by a Cutlass, the other boy appeared to have been shot through the body by a ball from a musket and one side of his head and down his face appeared to have been much cut by a Cutlass.

Another witness stated that 'on the other Native, near the jaw, the head was nearly severed from the body'.

Some of the accused were members of the party that had found the bodies of Hodgkinson and Wimbo and had been shocked at the gruesome appearance of the bodies. In their joint statement to the court, the accused referred to 'the Barbarous Cruel and Inhuman murder of the unfortunate Hodgkinson and Wimbo a murder the most horrid…' They further stated that anybody who had seen 'the mangled Bodies of the Deceased would have shuddered and even bore an antipathy against the cruel Natives in general, and that it behoves every man to be on his guard against them.' Clearly, the excessive violence perpetrated on the two victims was partly a response to the severe nature of the injuries that had been inflicted on Hodgkinson and Wimbo. Violence begets violence, and atrocities beget atrocities.

Another motive was retaliation and revenge. For instance, one of the accused stated that the two young Indigenous men had been killed 'at the request of Sarah Hodgkinson the widow of one Hodgkinson who had been killed by the Natives about three weeks before that time'. In fact, until 'widow Hodgkinson' protested 'not in my house', there was a strong possibility that the three men (one escaped) would be hanged from a beam in her house. Also, William Fuller, who was described as a resident of Richmond, 'a free man and lives by his Labor', was asked, 'Suppose any Natives should have come into your Farm after the above Expedition [to retrieve the bodies of Hodgkinson and Wimbo] would you have shot them?' Fuller replied, 'If I had seen any I suspected to have been concerned in the murder of said Hodgkinson and Wimbo I certainly should.'

On the Indigenous side, grievances apart from land theft were also mounting. For instance, when Hobby was asked why the natives would come down from the mountains to kill white people, including soldiers, as rumoured, he replied, 'I have heard it was in consequence of a native woman and child being put to death by a soldier called Cooper.' This, apart from other cases of depredations against Indigenous people, would have called for payback against white people. Further, Hobby was asked, 'Are not the Settlers or their Men in the habit of taking the women from the Natives and that the Native men are prevented taking them away through fear of Fire-arms?' He replied,

> In two instances I remember lately – but cannot say whether the Women were detained by force – but they were taken away against the inclination of their Native Men and I know that said two Women were common to the White Men from choice.

A further factor in the conflict, one that exacerbated the settlers' feeling of insecurity and their opinion that they had to take matters into their own hands, was their conviction that authority was not only distant but was also unresponsive, even unsympathetic, to their plight (see earlier). For instance, Lieutenant Hobby testified that he had gone to Sydney to tell the governor about an attack on a settler together with rumours that 'it was the intention of the Natives to come down in numbers from the blue Mountains to the Hawkesbury and to murder some of the white people and particularly some soldiers.' While he was in Sydney, he was told that 'Serjeant Goodall, a marine settler on the road between Parramatta and the Hawkesbury, whilst at work on his own grounds, had been attacked by several Natives, and so dreadfully wounded that his life was despaired of.' After Hobby imparted all this information, he asked the governor 'what was best to be done if the Natives persevered in committing such enormities'. The governor replied, 'something must be done,' to which Hobby responded that he intended, 'if the Natives should still continue such violent outrages, to send out a party of the military to kill five or six of them wherever they were to be found.' According to Hobby, the governor directed him 'to act discretionally against the Natives, leaving it entirely to me…'

The case of 'Charley' further illustrates what the settlers would have considered to be the dilatory response of the authorities. At the trial, a settler named William Goodall stated that

> about six weeks since he was working on his grounds when a party of Natives about Twelve in Number came up and without the least Provocation alarmed him by a desperate Attack with their Spears and also Brutally Beat him with their Waddies after wounding him in the breast and in two places in the Back with their Spears…

He managed to escape with a spear sticking out of his back. Goodall testified that one of his attackers was a man named Charley. A corporal of the New South Wales Corps testified that later he delivered Charley as a captive to Governor Hunter in Sydney, with a letter from Lieutenant Hobby that detailed Charley's offences. The corporal stated that

> His Excellency remarked it was not in his power to give Orders for the hanging or shooting of such Ignorant Creatures who could not be made sensible of what they might be guilty of, therefore could not be treated according to our Laws…

After some discussion of the case, 'the Governor then admonished said Charley as to his future conduct and ordered him to be discharged'.

Clearly annoyed by the governor's conduct, the corporal stated that 'he returned to the Hawkesbury and made report verbally to his Commanding Officer of what had been done, which he publicly repeated amongst the Settlers'. It was not a report that would increase confidence in authority among settlers who already felt exposed on the frontier of the settlement – more reason for taking matters into their own hands.

In this connection, there was confusion (whether wilful or circumstantial) about what settlers could, or could not, do. For instance, one of the accused stated that 'he understood it to be the Governors orders to kill the Natives where they found them'; he said that Hobby had repeated the instruction. However, Lieutenant Hobby said that 'he had given no such Orders nor did he believe the Governor had given any to that effect'. He explained that he ordered the soldiers who accompanied the party that went out to bury the bodies of Hodgkinson and Wimbo 'that if they fell in with any Natives on the road, either going or returning, to fire upon them'. In answer to a question from the court, Hobby said that several settlers had accompanied the soldiers, and that his orders 'to the party to go out and shoot any of the Natives they should meet' extended to the settlers. When asked if it was clear that his order only applied to that expedition, and to none other, he replied 'Such were the Orders I delivered to the Sergeant, but it is possible they might be misunderstood.'

Another factor exacerbating the conflict would have been the settlers' fierce determination to hold on to their land. Most of the settlers were former convicts or soldiers who would have had almost no chance of owning land if they had remained in their home country. Now they were richer and much more advantaged, comparatively speaking, than they had ever been, or ever could have hoped to be. In any case, where would they go, or what would they do, if they lost their land? The land was their wealth and their livelihood. It had been granted to them by the only authority that they recognised, and they would not be driven away easily.

The degree of alienation between the two races, at least in outlying districts of the colony, can be gauged from these words in the statement that the accused made to the court:

> It would be superfluous here to state the many Depredations which they [Indigenous people] Daily commit... It is well known by many of the Gentlemen Present that they are a Treacherous Evil minded Bloodthirsty set of Men, that they will be Familiar and be with People for a considerable time, until perhaps they have received 9/10ths of a Loaf of Bread and then for the last Tenth they will murder two or three who before were their friends to get it, many Instances of a similar kind are known.

The 'Hawkesbury case' provides a rare opportunity to get the views of 'ordinary settlers' about Indigenous people. As seen, the views were strongly negative: Indigenous people were accused of 'general inhuman behaviour', they were 'a Treacherous Evil minded Bloodthirsty set of Men', and they committed 'Barbarous Cruel and Inhuman murder'. Possibly, these views were extreme and one-sided because they emanated from armed conflict and from a situation where settlers were on trial for their lives. Nevertheless, many settlers in frontier districts would have felt the same; and when conflict subsided and the Indigenous threat had been subdued, the negative views and suspicions would have remained for a long time.

It was a common occurrence in colonial situations that, as the frontier expanded, outrunning the reach of authority, so settler security became more and more precarious. As a result, settlers often took matters into their own hands, for instance by forming commandos, militias, or self-defence organisations. The greater the distance between the settlers and Sydney, the weaker was the authority and sway of officialdom over their lives, and the more the settlers came to rely on their own resources and judgements. What Turner wrote about the American frontier was true of New South Wales as well; Turner observed, 'a system of administration was not what the West demanded; it wanted land'.

To repeat: rapprochement was only a hiatus in hostilities between settlers and Indigenous people and, moreover, it was restricted to a comparatively small area. In fact, within a short time, rapprochement was an anomaly rather than the norm. The reason was simple: as European settlements continued to expand, incorporating more and more land like an ever-rising tide, so did Indigenous resistance. Collins hit the nail on the head when he wrote,

> While they [Indigenous people] entertained the idea of our having dispossessed them of their residences, they must always consider us as enemies; and upon this principle they made a point of attacking the white people whenever opportunity and safety concurred.

Irrespective of what was said and what was done, this was the bedrock of the fraught relations between settlers and Indigenous people, namely that the settlers believed that they had a right to occupy and own the land, wherever and whenever they chose to do so, and Indigenous people resented the fact that their land was being stolen and tried to protect their 'country' wherever possible.

By 1791, Tench noted that some settlers had been armed 'for their protection against the natives'. The settlements were expanding far past the points where they could be securely protected by authority, and the situation became more volatile because the settlers, vulnerable and generally unmonitored, were armed. As Collins noted during 1794,

> The presence of some person with authority was becoming absolutely necessary among those settlers, who, finding themselves freed from bondage, instantly conceived that they were above all restrictions; and, being without any internal regulations, irregularities of the worst kind might be expected to happen.

He wrote this after a gruesome incident in which some settlers were reputed to have roasted a young Indigenous boy's back over a fire, and then thrown him into the Hawkesbury River, where they killed him with musket shots. Settler witnesses denied that the boy had been held over a fire and claimed that he was killed because he was a spy who was checking out the defences of the settlement.

Collins reflected the impotence of authority that strongly suspects wrongdoing but is unable to ascertain the facts when he wrote,

No person appearing to contradict this account, it was admitted as a truth; but many still considered it as a tale invented to cover the true circumstance, that a boy had been cruelly and wantonly murdered by them.

This resonates with the observation of Lichtenstein (1815) who wrote that although the 'trekboers' (nomadic farmers) of the Cape Colony were often responsible for atrocities, they were able to conceal themselves and their crimes from authority.

In addition, the authorities had lost control of firearms. During January 1796, Collins wrote that

> Several attempts had been made by the commissary to ascertain the number of arms in the possession of individuals; it being feared, that, instead of their being properly distributed among the settlers for their protection, many were to be found in the hands of persons who used them in shooting, or in committing depredations.

During the latest attempt to register all firearms in civilian possession, noted Collins, fewer than fifty out of 'between two and three hundred stands of arms which belonged to the crown' were tendered.

More arms were forthcoming for civilians: in a dispatch dated 2 March 1797, the Duke of Portland told Governor Hunter that a ship had departed with stores for the colony that included 'an hundred stand of arms [muskets with accessories] for the use of such of the inhabitants as you shall judge proper to be entrusted with them'.

In a dispatch dated 30 January 1802, Lord Hobart, Secretary of State for War and the Colonies, wrote to acting-governor King to express his displeasure at the state of race relations in the colony:

> I cannot help lamenting that the wise and humane instructions of my predecessors, relative to the necessity of cultivating the goodwill of the natives, do not appear to have been observed in earlier periods of the establishment of the colony with an attention corresponding to the importance of the object.

He lamented 'the evils resulting from this neglect' and, being perspicacious, noted that 'restoring confidence with the natives' would be difficult because they were 'alarmed and exasperated by the unjustifiable injuries they have too often experienced…' Lord Hobart added that resolving the matter was 'essential to the prosperity of the settlement' and advised that what he called the settlers' 'present dangerous embarrassment' would only be alleviated 'by observing uniformly a great degree of forbearance and plain, honest dealing with the natives…' He ended by wielding the big stick:

> It should at the same time be clearly understood that on future occasions, any instance of injustice or wanton cruelty towards the natives will be punished with the utmost severity of the law.

Governor King, no doubt resenting this high-minded missive from 17,000 kilometres away, reacted to Hobart's letter on 30 June 1802 by issuing a proclamation in which he noted that although the five men who been found guilty of 'wantonly killing Two of the Natives' had not been punished, 'It should, at the same time, be clearly understood that on future occasions any instance of Injustice or wanton Cruelty towards the Natives will be punished with the utmost severity of the Law.' The proclamation continued by stating that although 'His Majesty forbids any act of Injustice or wanton Cruelty to the Natives, yet the Settler is not to suffer his property to be invaded, or his existence endangered by them…' In defending their property, the settlers were 'to use effectual, but at the same time the most humane, means of resisting such attacks' and always to observe 'a great degree of forbearance and plain dealing with the Natives'. By so doing, 'the present good Understanding that exists' would be preserved.

Defend yourselves and your property, but do so humanely while displaying forbearance – what were the settlers to make of this set of incoherencies? And what was 'plain dealing'? Did it mean warning Indigenous people first, before you shot at them? Or something else?

If settlers ever heard of Lord Hobart's expostulations, they would probably merely have shrugged, remembering that London had pardoned the five men who were found guilty in the Hawkesbury trial, as referred to in Governor King's proclamation. Not only that, but they had never even been imprisoned: as Governor Hunter complained in a dispatch dated 2 January 1800 to the Duke of Portland, 'Those men found guilty of murder are now at large and living upon their farms, as much at their ease as ever.' It was all puff and huff from above, with nothing that commanded attention or obedience.

Also, Lord Hobart's words were much too late. The bird had flown the coop, and the horse had bolted from the stable. For almost fifteen years, Indigenous grievances had mounted as the colony appropriated lands and resources at an ever-increasing pace, while aggression and counter-aggression, accompanied by atrocities and fuelled by desires for revenge, had fuelled the 'state of war' about which Collins wrote during May 1795. Fine sentiments from colonial secretaries in London, and hand-wringing and expostulations from governors in Sydney, would not calm or reclaim the situation. The settlers wanted land, and they wanted protection when they had the land. If the state could provide protection, that was all too the good; if not, they would do it for themselves, by whatever means. The rest was waffle and background noise, worthy only of disdain. As for the Indigenous people – they should adapt or die.

Nine
Savage and inhumane

Hostilities between settlers and Indigenous people, and distance, spatially and administratively, between settlers and officials, were exacerbated by how rapidly the colony was expanding. For instance, on 26 November 1791, Tench noted, 'the number of persons, of all descriptions at Sydney, was 1259, to which, if 1628 at Rose Hill and 1172 at Norfolk Island be added, the total number of persons in New South Wales and its dependency will be found to amount to 4059'. The number of persons in the mainland settlements (2,887) was about twice the population that had landed with the First Fleet during January 1788, less than four years earlier. Significantly, as an indication of the rate of expansion, although Rose Hill/Parramatta was only founded during mid-1790, its population exceeded that of Sydney when Tench wrote one and a half years later.

Land was being appropriated and cleared at a rapid rate. For instance, during December 1790, Tench noted that near Parramatta, the superintendent of works 'estimated the quantity of cleared ground here at 300 acres… Six weeks ago this was a forest. It has been cleared, and the wood nearly burnt off the ground by 500 men, in the before-mentioned period, or rather in thirty days, for only that number have the convicts worked'. As already noted, when Phillip left the settlement during October 1792, 1,500 acres of land had been brought under cultivation. Comparatively speaking, this was a trifle because ten years later, one man, John Macarthur, owned more than double that number of acres (see later).

During 1802, when a French expedition visited Port Jackson, one of its members, M.F. Peron, gave an extensive account of Sydney, Rose Hill/Parramatta and adjoining areas. He noted that there were 'numerous flocks of excellent sheep' and commented that their wool

> was found to be superior to the rich fleeces of Asturias; and the English manufacturers pay dearer for it; because they are convinced of its superiority. This discovery will probably soon open to Great Britain, a branch of commerce as easy as it is lucrative.

He painted an idyllic picture of the country between Sydney and Parramatta, writing that

> Woods here and there open to the view, and the traveller perceives amidst them, spots which have been cleared by the settlers; and some of which are extensive: he discovers on them, many pretty habitations, shaded by beautiful trees...

He enthused that cattle, pigs, horses and poultry all flourished in these conditions.

Peron wrote that the population of Parramatta numbered between 1,400 and 1,500 persons, 'nearly all of whom are employed in the cultivation of land, the rearing of cattle, and the exercise of a few of the mechanical arts'. The town had 'about a hundred and eighty houses...' while the military barracks, 'capable of accommodating from two hundred and fifty to three hundred infantry' accommodated one hundred and twenty men of the New South Wales Regiment.

Peron was impressed with the capacity of the country for cattle and noted that

> in the divisions belonging to the state alone, there were...800 horned cattle, of which 514 were bulls, 121 oxen, and 1165 cows. The breeding of these animals is so rapid, that in the space of only eleven months, the number of oxen and cows has been extended from 1856 to 2450; which gives for the whole year an increase of 650 head, or one-third of the entire number.

However, the country was even more suitable for sheep, and Peron referred to 'Arthur [John Macarthur], one of the richest landholders in

New South Wales' who told him that 'in twenty years New Holland alone will be able to furnish England with all the wool which she now imports from other countries, and for which she pays annually about 1,800,000l. sterling'. Peron noted that Macarthur had more than 4,000 sheep on his farm of 3,400 acres 'of which 3160 are pasture, 40 sown with wheat, and the rest is occupied with various kinds of less important cultivation'.

Macarthur was not the only colonist who had 'derived in an honourable way the greatest advantages from the sheep of New Holland'. Peron wrote that 'Mr. Palmer has about 800 sheep, which he feeds on 392 acres of pasture. Mr. Marsden has a much greater number, and most of the other colonists have their particular flocks, wandering in the midst of woods, without enemies of any species...'

Considering that Macarthur arrived as a lieutenant and started with a grant of 100 acres during 1793, and Marsden, an Anglican clergyman, arrived in the colony during 1794, both had made good use of their time and opportunities during the intervening eight to nine years.

The ease with which deserving recipients could become landowners is shown in the following passage, which was written by a descendant of Samuel Marsden:

> In September, 1795, Captain Hunter arrived, and following in the steps of his predecessor, exerted himself in clearing land and bringing it under cultivation. To effect this he made a grant to every officer, civil and military, of one hundred acres, and allowed each thirteen convicts as servants to assist in bringing it into order. Mr. Marsden availed himself of the grant... Where land was to be had on such easy terms, it was not to be desired or expected that he should be limited to the original grant. He soon possessed an estate of several hundred acres – the model farm of New South Wales...

The land was there for the taking, and the only obstacle was the perverse hostility of some savages.

In addition to the Hawkesbury area, which experienced a lot of interracial conflict during the period from the mid-1790s until about

1816, other districts were also volatile, especially the stretch of country from Sydney to Parramatta, including Prospect Hill and Toongabbie in the Parramatta area. Expansion never stopped; for instance, this passage gives a flavour of the inexorable search for new land for settlements:

> Towards the latter end of the month, the Governor, accompanied by some gentlemen of the settlement, set off from Parramatta, on an excursion, in which he meant to obtain some knowledge of the ground between Duck River and George's River, with respect both to its quality and quantity. This tract was walked over, and much excellent land was found, well provided with fresh water in chains of large deep ponds. On this ground some of the marine corps, having completed their service, were desirous of being settled. (Collins, April 1797)

Indigenous people contested every area of new settlement, until they were driven away, killed, subjugated or, one senses, often succumbed to exhaustion and hopelessness. As early as August 1791, Tench wrote that 'a much larger party of the natives than had yet been seen assembled at any one time had destroyed a hut belonging to a settler at Prospect Hill, who would have been murdered by them, but for the timely and accidental appearance of another settler with a musket'. (Prospect Hill is about thirty kilometres west of today's Sydney CBD.) Phillip's response was to bolster defences by increasing the number of allotments and settlers in the area. The attack took place in the context of the latest expansion of the settlement: Tench reported that

> The governor had now chosen situations for his settlers, and fixed them on their different allotments. Twelve convicts, whose terms of transportation had expired, he placed in a range of farms at the foot of a hill named Prospect Hill, about four miles west from Parramatta; fifteen others were placed on allotments in a district named the Ponds...

Six months later, during May 1792, Collins noted that 'the natives had for some time been suspected of stealing the corn at the settlements beyond Parramatta'. He wrote that 'a party of the tribe inhabiting the woods, to the number of fifteen or sixteen' had been fired on while robbing a hut in Parramatta. It was supposed that one member of the party was wounded, because a few days later a convict was killed in brutal fashion. Collins wrote that the body had 'at least thirty spear wounds in it. The head was cut in several places, and most of the teeth were knocked out.' Indigenous people in Sydney said that this was probably 'revenge for the shot that was fired at the natives who some time before were stripping the hut'. In other words, it was payback.

By June 1792 Collins noted that

> The natives had lately become troublesome, particularly in lurking between the different settlements, and forcibly taking provisions and clothing from the convicts who were passing from one to another. One or two convicts having been wounded by them, some small armed parties were sent out to drive them away, and to throw a few shot among them, but with positive orders to be careful not to take a life.

During August 1792, Collins recorded that some convicts who had absconded into the bush, turned themselves in at Parramatta 'with an account of two of their party having been speared and killed by the natives'.

Between about 1792 and 1816, the accounts of hostilities are so numerous that I will only provide a sample here:

- 'About the latter end of the month a large party of the natives attacked some settlers who were returning from Parramatta to Toongabbie…' (Collins, December 1793)
- 'Between [Parramatta] and Prospect Hill some settlers had been attacked by a party of armed natives and stripped of all their provisions…it was noticed, that as the corn ripened, they constantly drew together round the settlers farms and round the public grounds, for the purpose of committing depredations' (Collins, January 1794)
- 'At Toongabbie, where the Indian corn was growing, their visits and

their depredations were so frequent and extensive, that the watchmen stationed for the protection of the corn-grounds were obliged to fire on them…' (Collins, March 1794)

- 'Pemulwy, or some of his party, were not idle about Sydney; they even ventured to appear within half a mile of the brickfield huts, and wound a convict who was going to a neighbouring farm on business.' (Collins, March 1795)
- 'We have no less than 700 men out of their time and off the public store, and we have many more whose time being nearly expir'd will be discharg'd if they desire it. Many of them have become a public and very dangerous nuisance; being too idle to work, they have join'd large bodys of the natives, and have taught them how to annoy and distress the settlers, who have many of them been murder'd by them, their houses burnt, and their stock destroyed… I am therefore oblig'd to arm the herds, and it distresses me to say that I fear I shall be under the necessity of sending arm'd parties in all directions to scower the country.' (Dispatch from Governor Hunter to the Duke of Portland, 20 June, 1797)
- 'From the wanton manner in which a large body of natives, resident about Parramatta, George's River, and Prospect Hill, have attacked and killed some of Government sheep, and their violent threat of murdering all the white men they meet, which they put into execution by murdering Daniel Conroy, stock-keeper, in a most savage and inhumane manner, and severely wounding Smith, settler…' (Government and General Orders, 1 May 1801)
- 'A detachment at George's River is to consist of a sergeant, corporal, and six privates until further orders… They are to fire on any native or natives they see, and if they can, pursue them with a chance of overtaking them' (Government and General Orders, 22 November 1801)
- 'In the vicinity of George's River several depredations have recently been committed by the Natives on the settlers stock, grain and other property.' (*Sydney Gazette*, 19 August 1804)

- 'The natives about Hawkesbury and Georges River still continue their depredations, the General order of the 27th of April is to continue in force respecting these places…' (Extract from Orderly Book 14 October 1804 to 8 January 1806)
- '…within these Three Weeks past, the Natives have been very troublesome among the distant Settlements at the South Creek and the lower part of the Hawkesbury River… I am sorry to say that until some of them are killed there is no hope of their being quiet.' (Dispatch from Governor King to Earl Camden, 30 April 1805)
- 'The Settlers etc. killed by the Natives were four, viz. Two Settlers and Two Stockmen – From the necessity of coercive Measures being taken, Six of the Reprisals Natives and those the most Guilty were Shot in a pursuit – I have therefore impressed on the Natives that altho' the Delinquents now in Custody ought to suffer, Yet as Two Black Men more than Settlers have been shot, I shall forego any farther retaliation…' (Dispatch from Governor King to Earl Camden, 20 July 1805)
- 'We are concerned to state that the natives have lately been very troublesome about the farms on the banks of George's River. Last week they plundered the ground of Mr. Strode; but were resolutely opposed by one servant and a neighbouring settler who came to his assistance… The articles of properly belonging to Henry Lamb, last week mentioned to have been fired by the natives and consumed, comprised his dwelling house, barn, a stack of barley, a cask of meat, household furniture, and whole wearing apparel of his family. (*Sydney Gazette*, 9 June 1805)
- 'Information has lately been received of an attack made by a party of the natives at Port Jervis upon Mr. Rushworth, master of the Fly colonial vessel, who received several spear wounds, from which he was recovering. Thomas Evans, one of the people who accompanied him, was unfortunately killed on the spot…' (*Sydney Gazette*, 8 December 1805).
- 'Last Thursday se'nnight a native banditti, 15 in number, attacked

the house of Joseph Marcus, on the Parramatta Road, and wounded his wife in the arm with a spear, got possession of two musquets, a quantity of ammunition, and robbed the house of a quantity of apparel and other property.' (*Sydney Gazette*, 24 September 1809)
- 'Last week a horde of the Branch natives beset a herd of swine beonging to Mr. Dyke, settler at the first Branch of the River Hawkesbury; of which they drove away three large pigs, and wantonly speared two very large sows, both of which died immediately of their wounds.' (*Sydney Gazette*, 20 June 1811)
- '…three privates of the Veteran Company, in the district of Appin, fired on a large body of the natives who were plundering the corn fields of a settler, and refused to desist, at the same time making use of every term of provocation and defiance, and in token of a determined spirit, menacing with their spears…' (*Sydney Gazette*, 14 May 1814)
- 'The hordes of Natives that shew themselves at a distance in the environs of the Cow Pasture Settlement, excite considerable alarm among the Settlers. Many of their wives and children have forsaken their dwelling, and sought shelter in securer places.' (*Sydney Gazette*, 4 June 1814)
- 'We have to regret the death of another white person, a stock keeper at the Cow Pastures; who was a few days since speared by three natives, who are reported to have come from the mountains in very alarming force, to join the nearer hordes in plundering the maize fields.' (*Sydney Gazette*, 16 March 1816)

Growing conflict was accompanied by growing disdain and alienation. We have seen that during the Hawkesbury trial of 1799, the statement by the five accused settlers described Indigenous people acerbically, as follows:

they are a Treacherous Evil minded Bloodthirsty set of Men, that they will be Familiar and be with People for a considerable time, until perhaps they have received 9/10ths of a Loaf of Bread and then for the last Tenth they will murder two or three who before were their friends to get it…

By the first decade of the nineteenth century, settler attitudes toward Indigenous people were becoming even harsher, if that were possible. The case of 'James Bath', which was reported in the *Sydney Gazette* of 2 December 1804, gives an insight into the bleak opinion that many settlers had of Indigenous people. 'James', who was described as 'a native youth who died at Sydney', was an orphaned boy who 'was rescued from barbarism by the event of his parents' death, both being shot while they were engaged in plundering and laying waste the then infant settlement at Toongabbee'. A prisoner named George Bath adopted him. When Bath's prison term expired and he left the settlement, James passed through the care of two other settlers before, at his request, he went to live with a third. With satisfaction, the *Gazette* reported of James that

> His origin he remembered with abhorrence, and never suffered to escape any occasion whereby he might testify a rooted and unconquerable aversion to all of his own colour – also esteeming the term Native as the most illiberal and severe reproach that could possibly be uttered.

The report lauded the deed that had 'snatched him from the habits of his countrymen' and reported with equal satisfaction that another Indigenous orphan, who had been 'baptised and received under the protection of the Rev. Mr. Marsden', also showed 'the same dislike to others of his own complexion as did the deceased'.

The views held by these two orphan boys tell us a lot about the attitude of many colonists toward Indigenous people. The boys' disdainful and negative views of their parents' race and culture did not develop out of nowhere: they could only have got their views from the colonists among whom they lived from infancy.

The newspaper continued by making a jingoistic meal of the short life of James Bath. It praised his skills and industrious habits, stating that 'with his early alienation from his sooty kindred' he had learned habits that were completely the opposite of those that characterised Indigenous people – he was

> docile, grateful, and even affable; he took much pride in cleanliness of dress, he spoke none but our language, and as he approached his latter end gave undoubted proofs of Christian piety…

Triumphantly, the report concluded that his example showed that 'the total indolence and inactivity of his countrymen is chiefly, if not entirely the effect of habit'; there was reason to hope that Indigenous people might yet learn to be industrious and useful.

In summary, the newspaper report depicted Indigenous people as barbaric, plunderers and ravagers, violent (that is, not 'docile'), ungrateful, unfriendly, dirty, linguistically deficient, pagan or irreligious, lazy, idle, and socially useless. However, there was some hope that Indigenous people might yet become useful, industrious, pious proletarians, fully subservient to the society that had colonised them.

The *Sydney Gazette and New South Wales Advertiser*, which began publishing during 1803, was the first newspaper published in the colony, where it had an almost completely clear run until 1824. The publisher was a convict, George Howe, who was also the government printer. Not surprisingly, Howe was only allowed to publish by permission of the governor, who ensured that every edition was censored. The masthead carried the words 'Published by Authority', and many editions carried lengthy official notices and proclamations. In a dispatch dated 9 May 1803, Governor King told Lord Hobart,

> it being desirable that the settlers and inhabitants at large should be benefitted by useful information being dispersed among them, I considered that a weekly publication would greatly facilitate that design, for which purpose I gave permission to an ingenious man, who manages the Government printing press, to collect materials weekly, which, being inspected by an officer, is published in the form of a weekly newspaper…

Key terms in the governor's dispatch are 'useful information' (the governor and his aides would decide what was 'useful' for settlers and inhabitants, and what was not), 'an ingenious man, who manages the Government printing press' (convict Howe had a comfortable and privileged position, which he would lose if he lost favour), and 'inspected by an officer' (in other words, censored by a trusted aide).

To what extent did the *Sydney Gazette* reflect the views of the majority of 'settlers and inhabitants'? Did most readers approve when the newspaper depicted Indigenous people as barbaric, plunderers and ravagers, violent, ungrateful, and so on? Significantly, the report about James Bath was not an exception; as will be seen, terms like these were often used in what passed for straightforward reports of events – that is, not in opinion pieces, editorials or letters to the editor. Also, the fact that the newspaper depended on subscribers to remain viable suggests that the publisher was confident that his readers would not object to the tone and content of the reports.

Also, because the newspaper was monitored, we can confidently assume that pejorative and judgemental language about Indigenous people was acceptable to the governor and his officials.

Both in public and privately, the governors led the way in using dismissive language to describe Indigenous behaviour. These are some examples:

- In a Government and General Order dated 1 May 1801, Governor King referred to 'the wanton manner in which a large body of natives, resident about Parramatta, George's River, and Prospect Hill, have attacked and killed some of Government sheep' and deplored the fact that they had continued by 'murdering Daniel Conroy, stock-keeper, in a most savage and inhumane manner.' The governor evoked sympathy for the settlers by contrasting the Indigenous peoples' 'hostile menaces' with the 'defenceless' state of the settlers.
- The orderly book of 19 April 1805 stated that 'the natives in different parts of the out settlements have in an unprovoked and inexcusable manner lately committed the most brutal murder of

some defenceless settlers' and further referred to 'the most barbarous treatment' that had been experienced by the settlers.
- In a dispatch dated 30 April 1805 to Earl Camden, Governor King contrasted the 'extremely liberal' behaviour of the settlers with the 'most ungrateful and Treacherous Conduct' of the natives. After describing a settler's death during an attack, the governor went on to say that 'Another Horror, but still more savage than the former, took place the same Day… The House belonging to a Settler was set on Fire by the same Band of Natives. After a search the mangled and burnt Limbs of the Settler and his Man were found, some in the Ashes and others scattered.' The governor referred to the incidents as 'These Barbarities.'

The fault was all on the side of the Indigenous people, who were depicted as having no reason except 'wantonness' for their aggression (which was 'inexcusable'), and were variously described as 'savage', 'inhumane', 'brutal', 'hostile', 'savage' and committing 'barbarities'. In fact, their unprovoked aggression was compounded by the fact that they were 'ungrateful' and 'treacherous' because they launched the attacks after they were given corn and other foodstuffs by the very settlers whom they attacked. On the other hand, the settlers were described as 'defenceless' and 'extremely liberal', while further sympathy was evoked by giving details of the 'mangled' state of the bodies. In fact, it was quite common to evoke sympathy for the settlers by describing the wounds and injuries that settlers suffered in attacks by Indigenous people. In almost all cases, the opposite, namely injuries suffered by Indigenous people, were only described when the writer intended to portray the intensity of in-group conflict, or the harsh ways in which Indigenous men treated women.

Through the reports in the *Sydney Gazette*, we can monitor the attitudes of settlers toward Indigenous people, remembering that the sentiments expressed in the newspaper had tacit approval of authority. Here is a sample for the period 1804–1814:

- A settler woman was 'treated with barbarity, unpardonable in the most savage race of men. The poor woman perceiving that they were driving her little flock of poultry off the ground, reproached them with their injustice, and fain would have rescued a portion of her property; but the unfeeling wretches turned their spears upon her, nearly twenty of which they threw, but happily without the intended barbarous effect.' The report continued, '…such is the treachery of those indolent and vicious hordes that infest the above neighbourhood, as to render useless and abortive every effort to maintain their friendship. By long intercourse many of them have acquired so much of our language as to understand and be understood, but only apply the talent to mischief and deception.' (19 August 1804)

- Escaped convicts whose stolen boat was wrecked north of modern-day Newcastle suffered as follows: 'after a series of unspeakable hardships they were assaulted by a body of natives, who showered spears upon them with a barbarity only to be conceived by those that have witnessed the brutal ferocity of these unfeeling savages,' (10 June 1804)
- '…they [Indigenous people] are also known to be ductile, and inclined to treachery: it consequently becomes every one to be upon his guard against surprise at all times; and not to place too implicit a degree of confidence in his friendly treatment…[from] an enemy who ships his spear without any provocation or pretext.' (3 March 1805)
- 'The above atrocities are for the most part confined to the hordes about George's River.' (15 October 1809)
- '…it is our undoubted duty to avoid every excitement to acts of hostility from these un-informed tribes, who, acting from momentary impulse upon all occasions, have it ever in their power to reek [sic] their vengeance upon the solitary unoffending settler, or the unguarded traveller. These considerations should restrain the civilized inhabitant even in cases where excessive provocasion [sic] might shelter him from the imputation of inhumanity.' (11 January 1812)

- '...those evils to which the lonely settler is exposed from the predatory incursions of an enemy whose haunts are inaccessible, distant, and unknown, and who by surprise or stratagem accomplish every project they devise in a wild temperament of fury natural to the savage state of Man.' (14 May 1814)

In a long article that was published in the *Sydney Gazette* on 28 July 1810, the author set out his understanding of the state of relations between settlers and Indigenous people. He noted that 'repeated skirmishes' had reduced the frequency of social contacts between settlers and Indigenous people, and said,

> Formerly our intercourse with the natives was much greater than at present; they frequented the settlements in numbers, and performed their exercises, most of which were hostile to each other, frequently among us; they were then familiar; almost everyone was known as well by an European name, which he assumed, as by his native appellation:- but that intimacy has subsided; for as the elders have fallen off, the younger, not receiving the encouragement of their parents met with upon our first acquaintance, seldom come among us...

The author speculated that one reason for the decreasing frequency of contact was that the Indigenous people had developed poorer opinions of the colonists. He deplored the fact that, rather than disapproving of Indigenous peoples' ceremonial conflicts and 'sanguinary cruelty', many settlers had enjoyed the spectacles, which reduced the esteem in which Indigenous people held them. In conclusion, said the author,

> ...in a few years more we may expect them totally to withdraw themselves from this part of the coast. Under such disadvantages, the civilization of these poor creatures must appear to be utterly impracticable until many obstacles are removed...

The author recommended that

> by acts of kindness we must obtain their friendship; we must endeavour to learn their language, and teach ours to as many of them

as possible, so as to enable us to converse with freedom, and to be perfectly understood to one another...

As usual, the author of this article was wishing for the impossible, namely that, even while Indigenous lands and resources were being taken forcibly by an ever-widening wave of settlement, the settlers could win over the oppressed people to friendship by 'acts of kindness' and so 'civilise' them. Presumably, only 'civilisation' would provide these 'poor people' with self-respect, dignity and the means of subsistence.

It is significant that the author referred to the fact that in the settlements there was decreasing interaction between settlers and Indigenous people. Also, it appears that the number of Indigenous people 'in this part of the coast' was decreasing so rapidly that soon they might disappear immediately. Was the number decreasing because land appropriation and aggression between the parties had driven the Indigenous people away from the occupied areas, or was it because, as has been claimed, the aggression had claimed the lives of so many Indigenous people? Had European-borne illnesses killed many Indigenous people? A combination of all of these? We don't know. However, there is speculation that many more Indigenous people died in the frontier conflicts than are numbered in the official reports.

Finally, Mann offered a somewhat different perspective on violence and relations between settlers and Indigenous people. He wrote that by 1808, 'The natives and our countrymen are now somewhat sociable, and there are not many outrages committed by either party.' However, he added that he was only speaking of circumstances in 'the vicinity of the principal settlements'. In more remote locations, things were different: '...they [Indigenous people] are still savages...' One reason for the peaceable relations, said Mann, was the death of Pemulwuy, who he termed 'a determined enemy to the Europeans'. However, the main reason was that

> an association with Europeans has in some degree polished their native rudeness, has softened the cruelty and natural violence of

their dispositions, and inculcated into their breasts some principles of humanity.

Mann continued by stating that Indigenous people had learned 'to discard a portion of that barbarity of manners, which allied them to the material creation'. The final words are especially significant; in them, Mann repeated the observation that, in their native state, Indigenous people were not much more than natural creatures. However, 'by observing the conduct of the new settlers', the Indigenous people had ascended to a higher state.

However, having claimed that being associated with Europeans had civilised the natives. Mann also wrote,

> but the proximity of a civilized colony has not tended in the least to polish the native rudeness and barbarism, which mark the behaviour of the original inhabitants of this remote spot of the universe.

Ten
A look at Bennelong and Pemulwuy

In many respects, Bennelong and Pemulwuy, who lived at the same time, were regarded so differently by settlers and authorities that they occupy opposite ends of the 'perception spectrum'.

Bennelong has a unique place in the early history of relations between colonisers and the colonised. During the period that I cover in this book, 1788–1816, much more was written about him than about any other Indigenous person. Also, unusually, in colonial records, where most Indigenous people are only called by their 'European' names, we have a record of Bennelong's other traditional names, namely Wollewarre, Boinba, Bunde-bunda and Wogetrowey. We even know quite a lot about his wife and his sister.

I will begin by restating some of the basic facts about Bennelong. He survived the devastating smallpox epidemic and possibly became a leader in a new group that formed from the survivors. During the period November 1789 to May 1790, he was captured, lived in the settlement, and then escaped. While he was in the settlement, Governor Phillip gave him special treatment, which included being on such intimate terms with the governor that they even called each other by the Indigenous terms for 'father' and 'son'. During this time, Bennelong learned a lot about European culture and ideas. Crucially, he also learned a lot about the colonizers' intentions for the infant settlement.

Towards the end of 1790, about six months after he escaped from the settlement, Bennelong arranged the payback spearing of Phillip. When Phillip did not seek revenge for this action, Bennelong led Indigenous people into the settlement, where he was accepted as a leader by both parties. This marked the end of hostilities between the settlers and the Indigenous people of the Harbour area. In gratitude, Phillip built a small house for Bennelong. From that time onwards, Indigenous people freely entered the settlement, where they were given special treatment.

In 1792, Bennelong and another Indigenous man named Yemmerrawanne travelled with Phillip to England. There, they were received as celebrities and met influential people. Yemmerrawanne died while in Britain, and Bennelong's health deteriorated.

Bennelong arrived back in Sydney on 7 September 1795. At first, affecting displeasure that his compatriots were not dressing and behaving like English men and women, he showed off the new ways that he had learned. However, it was not long before he returned to his old customs and habits. For instance, Collins reported that Bennelong would go about naked when he was with his compatriots, but would dress like a European when he dined at the governor's house. Also, when his wife died, Bennelong observed her passing in the traditional manner.

Until he died on 3 January 1813, although Bennelong continued to live in traditional manner, he was seen in and around the settlement. He appeared in the records a number of times, engaging in ritual combat, participating in payback, officiating at his wife's funeral and, on one occasion, being observed by Collins while he relaxed by the shore with his wife, her sister and their children, the adults dining on fish and oysters.

As I said, Bennelong got the attention of the colonial commentators in a way that no other Indigenous person did. Not even Arabanoo, the first Indigenous person to live in the settlement, got anywhere near the same attention. Bennelong was portrayed as a large and complex personality: physically impressive, effusive, intelligent, adaptable, passionate, quick to size up a situation, and shrewd. I will not repeat what I wrote earlier, except to emphasise that, at the time that he was captured, Bennelong had a leading position among the Indigenous people of the Harbour area. This was shown in many ways, one of which was that his compatriots were willing to support him in delivering payback on Governor Phillip.

Bennelong used his position to lead a significant number of the Indigenous people of the Harbour region into the settlement in an act that began rapprochement. From that time onwards, there was little, if any, aggression between the two groups. The European commentators were happy that hostilities had ceased now that the Indigenous people had been brought into subjection.

Although we know so much about Bennelong, there is also a lot that is not known. Partly, this is because from the time that Bennelong escaped from the settlement, we mainly see him as an actor in various dramas and events; and from those descriptions, including the tone in which they were written, we must try to piece together the perspectives of the writers and, dimly in the shadows behind them, the perspectives of their wider communities.

One of the biggest unanswered questions about Bennelong is why he led Indigenous people into rapprochement with the settlers. From the commentaries, it looks as if part of the reason was that it gave him personal satisfaction to show off his new acquaintances, skills and knowledge. As Tench wrote, Bennelong 'warmly attached himself to our society' because he was 'elated by these marks of favour, and sensible that his importance with his countrymen arose in proportion to our patronage of him...' After all, Bennelong was still a young man, about twenty-six years of age; as such, he was both impressionable and eager to make an impression.

However, if that was all that was at play, then he went far beyond what was required. As I noted earlier, by March 1791, about five months after Bennelong and his companions entered the settlement, Hunter wrote that 'the Natives being now become very familiar and intimate with every person in the Settlement, many of them now take up their rest every night in some of the Govt. [Government] houses'. Some Indigenous people became permanent inhabitants, while other were itinerant. Also, in many other ways, such as trading and employment, the Indigenous people became familiars of the settlement.

It is reasonable to infer that, having agreed a 'deal' with Phillip (and perhaps other senior officers), Bennelong led his people into subjection. Consider the situation: Bennelong was unique among all Indigenous people because of his close acquaintance with the colonialists, and especially from his favoured position with Governor Phillip. He could see that the Indigenous people were already greatly outnumbered – the huge death toll from disease had only exacerbated the imbalance – and he also understood that the colonialists were not only there to stay, but that more and more would be arriving, while the colony would appropriate ever more land and resources. Resistance was futile, because the colonialists had the technology, the weapons, the numbers, the back-up, and the resources to do what they wanted. Resistance would result in many Indigenous deaths and would only harden colonial resolve.

It is important to understand that Bennelong was not a coward. The records show several occasions on which he engaged in physical conflict in events such as payback rituals, ceremonial battles, and even one-on-one aggression. Often, his life was in danger, and he suffered several severe wounds. Also, there would have been other encounters that took place away from the gaze of the colonial note-takers. Nor did Bennelong lack other forms of courage, as seen, for instance, when he stood up to the all-powerful governor over the death of Bangai and on other occasions, transparently gave misleading information to protect his compatriots, Pemulwy and Willemering. It was not because Bennelong lacked personal courage and warlike skills, or other forms of courage, that he led his people into subjection. Rather, it was for strategic reasons, to give them some sort of future, even if it was as an oppressed people who inhabited their own country on sufferance of others. Despite being 'cabinned, cribbed, confined', survive they did…

From the time that he was captured until about the end of that year, 1790, there are many reports and descriptions of Bennelong, especially in the journals of Hunter, Tench and Collins. From them, it is possible to construct a comprehensive picture of attitudes toward him. Almost all of them were favourable. Among other qualities, he was portrayed as intelligent, personable, vivacious, adaptable, quick to size up situations, quick to seize opportunities, with impressive leadership qualities. However, after that, there is little information. There were two reports by Collins: one, via a message that was received while Bennelong was in England, stated that it was clear that he was missing his native country. The other, much longer report depicted Bennelong after his return to Sydney on 7 September 1795, where he showed off the customs and mannerisms that he had learned in England. Collins wrote approvingly,

> …every one who knew him before he left the country, and who saw him now, pronounced without hesitation that Bennillong had not any desire to renounce the habits and comforts of the civilized life which he appeared so readily and so successfully to adopt.

However, before long – we don't know how long – Bennelong had a physical altercation with a younger man concerning which of them should enjoy the attentions of his (Bennelong's) wife, who had defected during his absence overseas. After that, wrote Collins,

> His absences from the governor's house now became frequent, and little attended to. When he went out he usually left his clothes behind, resuming them carefully on his return before he made his visit to the governor.

Something happened to make Bennelong review his renunciation of his native culture.

During January 1796, Collins noted, 'Bennillong's influence over his countrymen not extending to the natives at the [Hawkesbury] river', there had been reports of violence between settlers and Indigenous people there. This was only five months after Bennelong returned from the long period away from home, and it appears that he had not lost standing in his group during that time. Six years later, during 1802, Peron also noted Bennelong's leadership when he wrote about 'the tribe of savages, called Gwea Gal, who acknowledge Bennil-long for their chief'. At about the same time, Joseph Holt, a convict and manager of a farm near Kissing Point, described Bennelong as 'the king of the natives' in the area; Bennelong's group apparently numbered from fifty to 100 people. (Kissing Point is on the water about halfway between modern-day central Sydney and Parramatta.)

Thanks to Keith Vincent Smith's article, 'Bennelong among his people' (2009), we have several references to contemporary observers who noted that Bennelong returned to his traditional customs and lifestyle soon after he returned from England. However, he visited the European settlements from time to time and enjoyed colonial products such as bread and other foodstuffs. According to the *Sydney Gazette*, which might not be trustworthy because it was no friend of Indigenous people, Bennelong also developed an excessive enjoyment of alcohol.

From the early 1800s until his death, Bennelong appeared several times in the *Gazette*, which carried condescending and scurrilous reports about him. For instance, under the title 'Native Amusements', the *Gazette* of 13 January 1805 carried the following item in mock heroic style:

> How would the pen of that great bard who sung the prowess of embattled Greeks upon Scamander's banks, recount the exploits of an artless band, whose dark exterior barely marks the cloud that dwells within, and scarcely leaves perceptible one human feature: except in manly courage. – Here Diomede, on either side appear… On Wednesday night the festival was given, in celebration of the approaching games; and as the ancient Bennelong was to withstand the torrent of revenge, a number of persons of the first respectability were present at the spectacle.

This was followed by an article dated 17 March 1805, in which it was reported how an Indigenous man accused of murder withstood a trial by combat:

> The spears of his adversaries were barbed and rough-glazed, and three at once advancing upon him until within ten or twelve feet, he caught the first thrown on his target, but the second, discharged by Bennelong, entered above the hip, and passed through the side so as to be afterwards extracted…

Mann deplored the fact that

notwithstanding so much pains had been taken for his [Bennelong's] improvement…he has subsequently taken to the woods again, returned to his old habits, and now lives in the same manner as those who have never mixed with the civilized world.

He noted that although Bennelong sometimes had 'intercourse with the colony', he preferred 'to taste of liberty amongst his native scenes' rather than to mix with 'strangers…however kind their treatment of him, and however superior to his own enjoyments'. In other words, although Bennelong had been shown a higher and better way, he had regressed to a lower state of being.

The report of Bennelong's death in the *Sydney Gazette* of 9 January 1813 is notorious for its dismissive, condescending venom. It stated,

Bennelong died on Sunday morning last at Kissing Point. Of this veteran champion of the native tribe little favourable can be said. His voyage to, and benevolent treatment in Great Britain produced no change whatever in his manners and inclinations, which were naturally barbarous and ferocious. The principal Officers of Government had for many years endeavoured, by the kindest of usage to wean him from his original habits, and draw him into a relish for civilized life; but every effort was in vain exerted, and for the last few has been little noticed. His propensity to drunkenness was inordinate; and when in that state he was insolent, menacing and overbearing. In fact, he was a thorough savage, not to be warped from the form and character that nature gave him, by all the efforts that mankind could use.

In summary, according to the *Gazette*, Bennelong was an inveterate, 'ferocious' savage who churlishly rejected the generous and 'benevolent' opportunities that he was given to better himself by becoming civilised. He was also an aggressive drunk.

Was this view peculiar to the *Gazette*, or was it widespread among the settlers? I don't know. The newspaper did not publish a rebuttal or dissenting view, so it looks as if its readers, at least, were in general agreement with the contents of the report.

Two aspects of the report are particularly interesting. The first is that Bennelong was described as a 'veteran champion of the native tribe'. This suggests that Bennelong did not merely 'slip back into' traditional habits and customs, but that he was an advocate for, and defender of, them. The second is that as a 'savage', Bennelong (and presumably all others of his ilk) were not included within the classification of 'mankind'. The British were the 'mankind' that had offered Bennelong the opportunities that he rejected, while by implication Indigenous people were of a different and lower order.

Writing during 1797, Collins expressed his bewilderment that

> It was distressing to observe, that every endeavour to civilize these people proved fruitless. Although they lived among the inhabitants of the different settlements, were kindly treated, fed, and often clothed, yet they were never found to possess the smallest degree of gratitude for such favours…

Collins was even more bewildered that their children, 'who had been bred up among the white people', returned to their native culture when they were adults. Collins concluded by noting sadly that even Bennelong was as susceptible as 'the most ignorant of his countrymen'.

Collins's ideas are worth unpacking. He said that the Indigenous people who were exposed to the advantages of 'civilisation', rejected it because they were ungrateful. The implication was that they were 'ungrateful' because, in some way, they lacked the ability to appreciate the advantages that they had been offered. Standing out head and shoulders among these ingrates was Bennelong, who rejected 'civilisation' in spite of having been feted and having enjoyed exceptional treatment as a captive, having been privy to the confidences of Governor Phillip, and having been granted the supreme favour of a visit to England, where he had been received by, and had mixed with, polite and cultivated society. Collins was bewildered: why would anyone who had been exposed to such favours and advantages, return to 'a savage mode of living, where the supply of food was often precarious, their comforts unworthy to be called such, and their lives perpetually in danger…?' Why, indeed?

Once more with thanks to Keith Vincent Smith's article, 'Bennelong among his people', we have further evidence that Bennelong was honoured among his own people. A traveller wrote a letter dated 17 April 1813 that was printed in the *Caledonian Mercury* in Edinburgh on 26 May 1814 in which was reported, 'Lately, in the vicinity of the town [Sydney], a battle took place, where about 200 were engaged, I believe in consequence of the death of the celebrated Bennelong...' This was no small funeral ceremony! Also, during 1821, Reverend Samuel Leigh showed a portrait of Bennelong to members of Bennelong's group. He recorded their reaction: 'When they looked upon his features, they were astonished, and wept aloud. "It is Bennellong!" they cried. "He it is! Bennellong! He was our brother and our friend!"'

In short, it looks as if, when circumstances catapulted Bennelong into the colonial centre and he gained a unique insight into the overwhelming force that had come upon his people and country, he decided not to 'kick against the pricks' but rather to do as advised by a character in Joseph Conrad's *Lord Jim*, namely, 'In the destructive element immerse yourself.' By doing so, he saved a portion of his people from further colonial violence and regained access to some of the country and resources that they had lost.

The colonial perspective changed during the years for which we have written records about Bennelong. At first, the officer-chroniclers depicted Bennelong in generally favourable terms. However, opinion changed when Bennelong largely rejected a Europeanised way of life and favoured traditional culture and customs. Then Bennelong was castigated for being an inveterate savage and ungrateful to boot, who had been shown the better way but inexplicably rejected the higher path and returned to a life of savagery and barbarism.

We know much less about Pemulwuy. Hunter provided the first reference when he wrote that when a colonial search party was looking for a missing convict, they came across Bennelong with a group of men, and 'Bannelong pressed them very much to return with him and kill a native who was well known from having lost an eye, and who was supposed to be a leader of the tribe that reside about Botany-Bay'. They refused the request. The reference was to Pemulwuy and the incident occurred during October 1790, soon after rapprochement began.

The next reference was two months later, when Pemulwuy killed McIntire at Botany Bay. Then, Bennelong and Colbee protected Pemulwuy and angered Governor Phillip by pretending that they would find Pemulwuy, when they had no intention of doing so, and gave misleading information to throw the search party off the track. This raises the question of what Bennelong's real attitude was towards Pemulwuy. Was he hostile toward Pemulwuy? Did he really want the soldiers to kill him? If there was hostility, was it because Pemulwuy denounced rapprochement as a surrender and a sell-out, and regarded Bennelong as the prime mover? This is possible and even likely. However, although the two were at loggerheads, it is likely that Bennelong protected Pemulwuy because his (Bennelong's) aversion to McIntire exceeded his dislike for Pemulwuy, and because blood was thicker than water. We don't know.

After the McIntire incident, Pemulwuy disappeared from the records until January 1795, when Collins noted that

> Two women (natives) were murdered not far from the town of Sydney during the night, and another victim, a female of Pe-mul-wy's party (the man who killed McIntire), having been secured by the males of a tribe inimical to Pe-mul-wy, dragged her into the woods...

We do not know which 'tribe' was hostile to Pemulwuy's people, and why. It is significant that although Collins named Pemulwuy as 'the man who killed McIntire', the colonial authorities did not try to bring him to colonial justice. The likely reason was that the authorities accepted payback as legitimate in relations between settlers and Indigenous people, even though they did not state it publicly.

Although Pemulwuy only appeared in the records sporadically, he was active in mobilising resistance to colonial occupation from the time that he killed McIntire during December 1790. This is attested by Collins, who wrote during March 1797 that ever since the death of McIntire, Pemulwuy 'had been a most active enemy to the settlers, plundering them of their property, and endangering their personal safety'.

During January 1795, Pemulwuy appeared in the records again when Collins reported that he attended an initiation ceremony in Sydney. Collins termed Pemulwuy 'a wood native', which indicates that he lived outside the borders of the colony. A few months later, during May 1795, Pemulwuy was directly implicated in aggression against settlers when Collins noted,

> Pemulwy, or some of his party, were not idle about Sydney; they even ventured to appear within half a mile of the brickfield huts, and wound a convict who was going to a neighbouring farm on business.

Later that year, during December 1795, Pemulwuy was so severely wounded in a clash with an escaped convict named 'Black Caesar' – Collins wrote that he was 'a savage of a darker hue, and full as far removed from civilisation' – that he was presumed dead. At the same time, Pemulwuy had wounded one of the Harbour Indigenous people with the European name of 'Collins'. We do not know the circumstances of this clash, but it could indicate ongoing hostility between Indigenous people who accepted rapprochement, and those who opposed it, like Pemulwuy.

Although he was wounded, Pemulwuy survived to lead the resistance. During March 1797, Collins wrote that Pemulwuy was 'a riotous and troublesome savage'. This was in the context of the 'Battle of Parramatta', where about 100 Indigenous warriors, led by Pemulwuy, advanced into Parramatta to attack the settlers and soldiers. Collins related that Pemulwuy,

> in a great rage, threatened to spear the first man that dared to approach him, and actually did throw a spear at one of the soldiers. The conflict was now begun; a musket was levelled at the principal, which severely wounded him. Many spears were then thrown, and one man was struck in the arm; upon which the superior effect of the fire-arms was shown them, and five were instantly killed.

Pemulwuy was captured and taken to hospital with severe wounds. Despite shackles and wounds, he escaped.

A month later, when the governor was exploring land around George's River and Botany Bay with a view to opening it for settlement, members of the his party

> met with several parties of natives, among whom was Pe-mul-wy, who, having perfectly recovered from his wounds, had escaped from the hospital with an iron about his leg. He saw and spoke with one of the gentlemen of the party; enquiring of him if the Governor was angry, and seemed pleased at being told that he was not; notwithstanding which, there could be but little doubt that his savage brutal disposition would manifest itself whenever excited by the appearance of an unarmed man.

Hostilities continued and Collins said that the settlers at Lane Cove, which is only about ten kilometres from today's central Sydney, were 'perpetually alarmed' at the prospect of being attacked. The situation became so desperate that the governor threatened that 'any of the natives [who] were taken in the act of robbing the settlers' would be hanged 'in chains near the spot as an example to others'. In reporting this situation, Collins expressed the opinion that it would have been better to have driven Indigenous people far away from the settlements because the existing situation was caused by 'the kindness which had been shown them [Indigenous people], and the familiar intercourse with the white people in which they had been indulged'.

During May 1797, Collins reported that 'The natives, ever hostile to the settlers, had lately killed one of them: these natives belonged to the tribe of which Pe-mul-wy was the leader.' A year later, during March 1798, he wrote that

> A strange idea was found to prevail among the natives respecting the savage Pe-mul-wy… Both he and they entertained an opinion that, from his having been frequently wounded, he could not be killed by our fire-arms.

Collins commented further that because of Pemulwuy's presumed immunity to firearms, 'he was said to be at the head of every party that attacked the maize grounds'.

Pemulwuy's long-term strategy was not only for his warriors to attack individuals, but also to steal and destroy maize and wheat. The latter was especially important to the survival of the colony; for instance, during December 1793, Collins referred to the dire shortage of flour in the colony as 'total deprivation of so valuable, so essential an article in the food of man…' A year later, he wrote, 'To lose the seed-wheat would be to repel every advance which had been made toward supporting ourselves, and to crush every hope of independence.' The situation escalated to the point where the governor issued a Government and General Order on 22nd November 1801 by which a military detachment was posted at George's River 'to prevent the natives from firing the wheat'. The soldiers were instructed 'to fire on any native or natives they see, and if they can, pursue them with a chance of overtaking them. Every means is to be used to drive them off, either by shooting them or otherwise…' Similar orders were given to a detachment at Parramatta.

Further, the governor offered a reward, dead or alive, for two escaped convicts who were in league with the Indigenous warriors, together with Pemulwuy; the three were described as 'the promoters of the outrageous acts that have been lately committed by the natives, whereby two men have been killed, several dangerously wounded, and numbers robbed…'

In a dispatch to Lord Hobart dated 30 October 1802, Governor King reflected on the seriousness of the security situation from the colonial point of view when he stated that

> the natives having shown a disposition to become troublesome to the settlers…soon after plundered many of the settlers, wantonly murdered four white men, and cruelly used some of the convict women at different times.

The natives 'in the neighbourhood of Parramatta and Toongabbee… were irritated by an active, daring leader named Pemulwye…' King explained that after he offered a reward for Pemulwuy 'either dead or alive', two settlers shot and killed him. Next, said King, some Indigenous people

> requested that Pemulwye's head might be carried to the Governor, and that as he [Pemulwye] was the cause of all that had happened, and all anger being dropped on their part, they hoped I would allow them to return to Parramatta

The next mention of Pemulwuy in official correspondence was in a dispatch dated 5 June 1802 from Governor King to Sir Joseph Banks, in which King referred to the fact that he was sending Pemulwuy's head to Banks. King knew that Banks would be happy to receive the gift because 'the possession of a New Hollander's head is among the desiderata [that is, desirable objects].' He explained that he had 'put it in spirits and forward it by the [ship named] *Speedy*.' He added, 'The printed paper will explain how I came by the head. The bearer of it you will find mentioned in Collins's books.'

Unlike Bennelong, Pemulwuy at least got an official obituary of a sort. In his letter, Governor King said this about Pemulwuy: 'Altho' a terrible pest to the colony, he was a brave and independent character.'

As far as we can tell, the settlers had similar views of Bennelong and Pemulwuy. Both were regarded as inveterate barbarians and savages. However, possibly Bennelong was viewed even more harshly on the grounds that he was an ingrate who, despite having been given unique privileges and opportunities to understand the colonial culture and become 'civilised,' rejected it in favour of his native culture and way of life.

In one of his essays (I forget which one), Chinua Achebe used the fable of the oak and the reed to contrast different responses of the colonised to colonialism. In the fable, the oak stands strong and immovable against all storms and buffeting, until finally one storm proves to be too great, and it is uprooted and topples over. On the other hand, although the reed sways this way and that as the winds blow and the storms rage, it is never uprooted and always returns to an upright position.

Pemulwuy was the oak and Bennelong was the reed.

Eleven
The civilising mission

The royal commission given to Lachlan Macquarie, governor from 1810 to 1821, resembled the one that was given to the earlier governors. Regarding the Indigenous people, Macquarie was instructed 'to extend your Intercourse with the Natives, and to conciliate their Affections, enjoining all Our Subjects to live in Amity and Kindness with them'. Anyone who 'wantonly destroy[ed] them', or interfered with them in the course of their occupations, should be punished. Also, Macquarie was instructed to report how many natives lived in and about the settlements, and to state 'in what Manner the Intercourse with these People may be turned to the Advantage thereof'.

The autocratic Macquarie was in a hurry to put his stamp on the young colony. Among his early tasks, even while sorting out the chaos that had been caused by the 'Rum Rebellion' against Governor Bligh, were to approve the street layouts of Sydney and Hobart, to order public buildings in Sydney, to reform the currency system, and to bring freed or 'emancipated' convicts into the administration. He also presided over a burst of exploration, as well as expansion of the colony's borders, at a time when the settler population, and hence demand for land, was growing rapidly.

On 15 December1810, less than one year after he took up his position as governor, he proclaimed five new 'townships', which included 'one for the Nepean, or Evan District, to be called Castlereagh'. After an account had been given of existing settlers and their livestock in the districts, stated Macquarie, he would 'instruct his Acting Surveyor to mark out the several Allotments to enable the Settlers to commence with the least possible delay the business of erecting Houses and removing thither'.

On 6 November 1810, Macquarie began a journey to inspect the interior of the colony. As recorded in his journal, expansion was on his mind. At one point, he noted,

> having rode between 14 and 15 miles through the best and finest Country I have yet seen in the Colony… I intend forming this Tract of Country into a new and separate District for the accommodation of small Settlers, and to name it 'Airds' in honor of my dear good Elizabeth's Family Estate!

Later in the trip, they passed along the right bank of the Nepean River where, he noted,

> appeared a very fine rich Soil fit both for Tillage and Pasturage. Thence we passed through a long extensive chain of Farms along the Nepean… These are all good Farms, good Soil, and well cultivated…

The expansion of the colony into areas south and west of Sydney around the Nepean River would soon have severe consequences for relations with Indigenous people.

Macquarie employed a carrot and a stick approach toward Indigenous people. The carrot was his project 'to effect the Civilization of the Aborigines of New South Wales and to render their habits more domesticated and industrious'. In this, Macquarie was in tune with 'advanced' Europeans' views about how to deal with natives in the colonies; as Knapman and Müller observed, 'The idea of reforming natives by advancing them up the stage of civilisation was a recurring theme in late eighteenth and early nineteenth century British colonial thought in Southeast Asia.' Although Indigenous people might have thought that this was not a carrot worth having, Macquarie was much taken with his initiative.

The stick was his proclamation of a state of emergency and his ruthless use of military force. In a dispatch dated 18 March 1816 to Lord Bathurst, Macquarie set out his dual approach succinctly:

I am Still determined to persevere in My Original Plan of endeavouring to domesticate and Civilize these Wild rude People. In the mean time it will be Absolutely Necessary to Inflict exemplary and Severe Punishments on the Mountain Tribes who have lately exhibited so Sanguinary a Spirit against the Settlers.

The ground for the 'civilising' project was prepared by a three-part article in the *Sydney Gazette*, which was published between 14 July and 4 August 1810. Significantly, the whole article ran to more than 2,200 words, which was a generous allocation of paper at a time when supplies sometimes ran short. Almost certainly, the articles were a plant by Governor Macquarie to prepare the colonial public for his 'civilising mission' for Indigenous people. Even if Macquarie did not pen the articles himself, there is no doubt that he stood four-square behind them.

The governor's plant began with a 'Query' under the pen-name 'Philanthropus'. It was published on 7 July 1810 and was addressed 'To the PRINTER of the SYDNEY GAZETTE.' It invited a response and began by stating that 'the great Creator' had made 'of One Blood all Nations of the Earth'. (Although it is doubtful that many colonists agreed with this assertion, no one was impolite enough to lodge an objection, at least not in the columns of the newspaper.) The Query continued by saying that it took 'for granted that the Natives of New South Wales are capable of instruction and civilization'; that being the case, it asked, 'What plan can be adopted, what means used, or what steps taken, whereby we may most speedily and effectualy civilize and evangelize the Natives of New South Wales, local circumstances considered?'

In reply, the first article detailed the barbarism of the Indigenous people and concluded that 'the adults of our native tribes are beyond the present reach of civilisation…' The second article recommended that a 'friendly intercourse' between settlers and Indigenous people should be re-established by 'encouraging their visits to the settlements, by acts of kindness'. In particular, the civilising project required that 'As many of their children as they can be prevailed on to part with, must at an early age be distributed among the families of sedate persons.'

Next, 'they should be sent to school, at which the teacher must be careful to prevent the white children from making any improper reflexions on their colour, or treating them in any other way contemptuously.'

The third and final article expressed anxiety about mixing the races in the schoolroom and partially backtracked on the former article by observing that 'an indiscriminate inter-mixture with our own children, which in other respects would certainly be advisable, might tend to retard rather than to accelerate their progress.' The reason was that 'there are numbers in our own Community who affect to despise the character of a Heathen, and are yet too faulty in themselves to attend to the duties that characterize the Christian'. This gave the author the cue to embark on a homily about cultivating and improving virtuous conduct, which included the injunctions

> that instead of contriving to evade we should assist in the enforcement of the laws by which we are governed; that we should learn temperance, and obedience to our superiors [*sic*]; that our religious duties should be more especially an object of regard, and that by a rational intercourse among each other, we should charm the barbarian rather than disgust him at our failings…

Observance of the law, practising temperance, obeying superiors and practising religion: these were qualities that were close to Macquarie's heart.

It was proposed that 'in their infancy', Indigenous people should be

> treated tenderly, in order that as they grow up they may look back with aversion to the hardship of their primitive condition, and feel the more sensibly their obligations to Providence, and to us as its immediate instrument, in relieving them from a state of misery and want.

By so doing, they would become 'accustomed to ease, comfort, and security', which would attach them to European society, where they would learn that 'a life of industry' was necessary to continue to enjoy the civilised existence to which they had become accustomed.

The articles are useful as a record of perspectives on Indigenous people after twenty-two years of colonisation. Nothing much had changed. The 'Natives of New South Wales' were still regarded as being in a 'deplorable state of barbarism' from which Europeans could 'rescue' them. They were 'too indolent to provide for their common wants', an instance being their habitual nakedness, which showed that they were so lazy that they could not even protect themselves from the extremes of weather 'which they nevertheless acutely feel'. Because they did not cultivate 'a single herb or plant', they had to rely on chance to provide them with sustenance. One result was that 'they indiscriminately devour the most loathsome insects, with the most nauseous filth, that can with the least trouble be obtained'. However, Europeans had learned that it was futile to try to 'civilise' Indigenous people in the way that had previously been tried, because they always turned their back on European culture and habits and returned to their roots. The lesson was that the only hope of 'civilising' them lay in influencing them from a very early age.

In a letter written during March 1816 (no date), a free settler, Mrs John Macarthur, expressed similar views that would have been widely representative. She wrote, 'Attempts have been made to civilise the natives of this country, but they are complete savages, and are as lawless and troublesome as when the Colony was first established.' A year later, on 8 March 1817, she associated the natives with the animal life of the colony when she wrote,

> All the animals and plants hitherto discovered are entirely new, and differ from the productions of any other known land. The inhabitants resemble the natives of this district. They are a singular race utterly ignorant of the arts, living constantly in the open air, and without any other covering than occasionally, cloaks of the skin of wild animals…

This, too, was a view that would have been widely held in the settler community.

On 28 October 1810, Macquarie informed the Earl of Liverpool, Secretary of State for War and the Colonies, that he was forwarding under cover 'for Your Lordship's Information, a Series of the *Sydney*

Gazettes from the 7th of May (when last Sent) to the 20th Inst. Inclusive.' Among other initiatives, Macquarie wanted his superiors to know what he was preparing by way of the civilising project. We don't know what the Earl of Liverpool made of this bundle of newspapers from a distant colony that arrived nine months or more after publication. Very likely, the newspapers didn't get anywhere near the earl's desk.

The civilising project was on display at a ball at Government House that was held on 18 January 1811 to celebrate the queen's birthday. The *Sydney Gazette* of 19 January reported that the north end of the ballroom was covered with a transparent painting that represented 'our Native Race in their happy moments of festivity…instead of expressing dissatisfaction at the humility of their condition, earnestly anticipating the blessing of civilization…' The painting included 'a striking full-sized figure' of an Indigenous man who was pointing at the Church of St Philip, 'of which an accurate perspective view was given, as symbolical of the Christian Religion inviting them to happiness…'

As exemplified in the ballroom painting, Macquarie believed that rigorously observing 'religious duties' was an essential component of 'civilisation.' For instance, in the Query (see above), the words 'civilise and evangelise' collocate as mutually reinforcing qualities. On 27 October 1810, Macquarie 'rejoiced' to report to the Earl of Liverpool that during the short period that he had been governor, there was

> a very apparent Change for the better in the Religious Tendency and Morals of All the different Classes of this Community. Persons of all religious Persuasions and Descriptions attend Divine Worship on Sundays, and I have all the Convicts of both Sexes here, and at the different Dependencies, mustered every Sunday Morning, and Marched to Church in their best Clothes under the Direction of their respective overseers and Superintendants [*sic*].

Major General Macquarie, who ordered that the convicts should be mustered and marched to church in their best clothes every Sunday, would have approved of the words and sentiments of the hymn 'Onward Christian Soldiers'. If the hymn had been written sixty years earlier, singing it would have been a bracing accompaniment as the ordered ranks marched to church, there to improve their morals and their respect for authority, both divine and secular.

From time to time, Macquarie assured his superiors in London that everything in the colony, including the natives, was quiet and orderly. However, this was painting the situation rosier than it was, because he had to deal with ongoing unrest as well as a major insurrection halfway through his period of service. Although Indigenous resistance around the Hawkesbury region had largely been eliminated by the time that Macquarie arrived, relations in the region were still sensitive.

On 20 June 1811, the *Sydney Gazette* reported,

> Last week a horde of the Branch natives beset a herd of swine belonging to Mr. Dyke, settler at the first Branch of the River Hawkesbury; of which they drove away three large pigs, and wantonly speared two very large sows, both of which died immediately of their wounds.

Of course, the spearing was not 'wanton', but rather was deliberate, as an expression of anger and frustration. Further, on 9 January 1813, the newspaper reported that a settler had been killed at Portland Head on the Hawkesbury River: 'The perpetration of the horrible offence is attributed to several natives, said to belong to the Lower Branch…'

On 11 January 1811, the *Gazette* reported that 'a party of Natives' had complained to the Chief Constable at Windsor that 'one of their tribe had been fired at and supposed to be killed at Richmond'. The newspaper reported that the chief constable investigated the matter and, although

> no traces were visible that could give colour to the information… a white man and woman were taken in to Windsor, where, as stated by the latest accounts from thence, they awaited an investigation of the challenge.

The newspaper went on to express the hope that there was no truth in the accusation,

> as it is our undoubted duty to avoid every excitement to acts of

hostility from these uninformed tribes, who, acting from momentary impulse upon all occasions, have it ever in their power to reek [*sic*] their vengeance upon the solitary unoffending settler, or the unguarded traveller.

That being the case, cautioned the newspaper, the 'civilized inhabitants' should be careful not to provide any reason for provocation.

However, it was in southern parts of the colony around the Nepean River that the smouldering coals were being flamed. On 7 May 1814, the *Gazette* reported,

> The mountain natives have lately become troublesome to the occupiers of remote grounds. Mr Cox's people at Mulgoa have been several times attacked within the last month, and compelled to defend themselves with their muskets… On Sunday last Mr Campbell's servants at Shancomore were attacked by nearly 400… Similar outrages have been committed in other places; which it is to be hoped will cease without a necessity of our resorting to measures equally violent to suppress the outrages.

A week later, deploring the collapse of 'the tranquillity and good understanding that for the last 5 or 6 years has subsisted', the newspaper carried an extensive report about violent incidents in the southern region of the colony. In the Appin district, two farms were attacked and one settler was killed, while on the Indigenous side, at least one man, one woman, one boy, and two children were killed. The next day, the attackers killed a settler man and woman. The newspaper said that it was ominous that the indigenous people 'of the mountains' were no longer visiting 'the settlements of the interior'. The reporter did not know whether this was 'with a view to their own security, or for the purpose of alarming the yet more distant inhabitants…' Whatever the reason, travellers should be cautious because they were 'liable in a moment to be surprised and surrounded from the sides of the roads, and subjected to very ill, most likely barbarous treatment'.

In a letter dated 16 May 1814, settler Hannibal Macarthur informed his uncle, John Macarthur, about events at Cowpastures, saying that 'The

Natives have become extremely troublesome and amongst others we have become sufferers in the Death of a Shepherd's wife and your old favourite Wm. Baker who were inhumanly murdered...' Hannibal was dismissive of Governor Macquarie's ability to deal with the situation, saying that although he had informed him about 'this horrid event', the governor was 'so much taken up with a Parade of a garrison' that he could not defend or protect the distant parts of the colony. Hannibal Macarthur's frustration with Macquarie probably reflected the views of many colonists, especially those on and near the frontiers, who would have wanted vigorous action to defend persons and property and would have had little patience with ideas about civilising and evangelising the natives.

Ominously, on 4 June 1814, the *Sydney Gazette* reported that

> The natives of Jarvis's Bay are reported in good authority to have coalesced with the mountain tribes; they commit no depredations on the corn fields, but have declared a determination, that when the Moon shall become as large as the Sun, they will commence a work of desolation, and kill all the whites before them...

This suggested that a line of Indigenous resistance stretched from the mountains, across the southern frontier of the colony, and all the way to the Illawarra–Jervis Bay area (as it is called today). In this regard, earlier on 4 January 1812 a boat crew reported that at the Shoalhaven River, which is about halfway between the Illawarra and Jervis Bay, they had to exercise 'active vigilance' for 'their protection against the natives, who appeared to be numerous and athletic'. On 4 June 1814, the newspaper reflected that 'The natives of Jarvis's Bay have never been otherwise than inimical to us; for small vessels have never touched there without experiencing their hostility in some degree or other.' Later, on 25 February 1815, it was reported that native people had killed three crew members of an open boat at the Shoalhaven.

Also, on 4 June 1814, the *Gazette* reported,

> The hordes of Natives that shew themselves at a distance in the environs of the Cow Pasture Settlement, excite considerable alarm

among the Settlers. Many of their wives and children have forsaken their dwelling, and sought shelter in securer places.

The situation had become so insecure, stated the same report, that the settlers in the Appin area had formed a self-defence militia,

> comprising 8 or 10 settlers of the district; who alternately keep a night watch, and are intent on making the best defence practicable, in case of attack; and if hard pressed by their assailants, who appear to have less dread of fire arms than formerly, they retire upon the district of Airds, which being more numerously settled, will be capable of affording them a shelter.

The phrase 'if hard-pressed' suggests that the settlers anticipated that they could be dealing with more than just occasional or sporadic attacks.

Violence continued. Two weeks later, the newspaper reported,

> A body of natives on Wednesday last in the forenoon attacked and killed two of Mr. Broughton's servants, at his farm in the district of Appin… A shepherd has been reported missing, who we hope may be in safety.

Confrontations continued along the southern bounds of the colony; on 5 August 1815 the *Gazette* reported that 'a body of natives between 30 and 40 in number' had wounded a man and his wife near Bringelly and had stolen items from their hut. This was followed by a report dated 9 March 1816 that stated, 'Unpleasant accounts are received from the farm of Captain Fowler, in the district of Bringelly, of the murder of several persons by the natives frequenting that quarter.' This was a fierce and resolute battle; the newspaper reported that when the pursuing party got bogged down in marshy ground, they were

> immediately encircled by a large body of natives, who closing rapidly upon them, disarmed those who carried muskets, and commenced a terrible attack, as well by a discharge of the arms they had captured, as by an innumerable shower of spears. M'Hugh, Dennis Hagan, John Lewis, and John Murray, fell in an instant, either from shot, or by the spear, and William Brazil received a

spear in the back between the shoulders, which it is hoped and believed will not be fatal. Some of the natives crossed the river over to Capt. Fowler's farm, and pursued the remaining whitemen up to the farm residence...

Houses and property had been destroyed and some property had been carried away.

A week later, on 16 March 1816, the newspaper reported,

We have to regret the death of another white person, a stock keeper at the Cow Pastures; who was a few days since speared by three natives, who are reported to have come from the mountains in very alarming force, to join the nearer hordes in plundering the maize fields.

Two weeks later, the newspaper reported that

an attack was made by a body of natives upon the farm of Lewis, at the Nepean, whose wife and manservant they cruelly murdered. The head of the unfortunate woman was sever'd from the body, and the man was dreadfully mangled with a tomahawk. The furious wretches afterwards plundered the house, and wantonly speared a number of pigs...

Another attack had been made on farms around Lane Cove, which was much closer to Sydney town.

The newspaper reflected that in 'their mischievous and truly horrible incursions', the Indigenous warriors always attacked in overwhelming force, and then retreated to secluded positions where it was difficult to follow them. The newspaper also said, 'these hordes are known to belong, mostly, if not all, to the more retired tribes' – in other words, they represented Indigenous groups whose territory had not yet been colonised. This suggests that these 'retired tribes' had noted the fate of other groups that were closer to the colony, or had been overtaken by the colony, and had decided to take pre-emptive action to try to maintain their independence and territorial integrity.

At the same time, Macquarie's civilising project was proceeding apace. During April 1814, William Shelley, resident at Parramatta, who had been both a missionary and a businessman, proposed an Indigenous educational institution. Macquarie encouraged him, and on 20 August 1814, Shelley submitted a comprehensive plan, with him as the manager of the institution. The first point of the nine-point plan was 'That there be a Native Institution to consist of a Committee of Five Persons under the Governor, as Patron, Mrs. Macquarie, as Patroness.' The object of the institution would be 'the Civilization of the Natives of New South Wales'; Native children of both Sexes would be enrolled, to be taught 'Reading, Writing, etc., also useful occupations, as Agriculture, Mechanical Arts, and such Manufactures as may best suit the Age and disposition of the children…'

Not surprisingly, given the amount of groundwork that had been done, Macquarie accepted the idea. His dispatch dated 8 October1814 to Earl Bathurst included Shelley's plan and stated,

> I have determined to make an Experiment towards the Civilization of these Natives, Which is the Object I have in View by this Address, and trust it Will Meet Your Lordship's benevolent Patronage.

Macquarie began the dispatch with a long disquisition on the natives of New South Wales in which he described them as an 'Uncultivated Race of aborigines' and said that they had 'Scarcely Emerged from the remotest State of rude and Uncivilized Nature…' Nevertheless, they had some qualities which, 'if properly Cultivated and Encouraged, Might render them not only less wretched and destitute…but progressively Useful to the Country According to their Capabilities either as Labourers in Agricultural Employ or among the lower Class of Mechanics'. With time, patience and friendship, it would be possible to bring these

> Unenlightened People into an important Degree of Civilization, and to Instil into their Minds, as they Gradually open to Reason and Reflection and a Sense of the Duties they owe their fellow Kindred and Society.

On 18 June 1814, Macquarie issued a general order in which he expressed his regret in having to advert to the unhappy Conflicts which have lately taken place between the Settlers in the remote Districts of Bringelly, Airds, and Appin, and the Natives of the Mountains adjoining those Districts; and He sincerely laments that any Cause should have been given on either Side for the sanguinary and cruel Acts which have been reciprocally perpetrated by each Party.

His regret would have been genuine: the frontier confrontation, and the military response to it, exposed the vacuity of Macquarie's 'civilising project'. Next, Macquarie proceeded to a lengthy disquisition on the rights and wrongs on each side, and advised that the settlers should 'exercise their Patience and Forbearance, and therein [to] shew the Superiority they possess over those unenlightened Natives…' He gave the assurance that any further incidents would be the subject of 'minute Enquiries,' and that the guilty parties on both sides would be punished.

Less than one month later, on 9 July 1814, in a further attempt to cool inflamed settler passions, the *Sydney Gazette* carried an article that began by expressing the hope that the measures that had been adopted by the governor would re-establish 'the good understanding, between the natives and ourselves, which has subsisted during the whole period of his Government…' The article then described the difficult conditions under which Indigenous people lived, stating that

> They are without houses, without cloathing [*sic*], and how they subsist at all must be a matter of wonder to a people whom the arts have happily instructed to render the fields obedient to their needs, and everything in nature tributary to their wants. They have neither flocks nor herds…

In conclusion, the writer stated that, while maintaining security,

> it would be highly praiseworthy in British Settlers to exercise their patience and forbearance, and therein shew the superiority they possess over the unenlightened Native.

Governor Macquarie was appealing to the settlers to exercise patience and to give him a chance to develop an amicable solution to the conflict. It was not to be.

One of Macquarie's responses to the escalation of confrontation was to consolidate his plans for the 'civilising' of the Indigenous people. In a pronouncement dated 10 December 1814, he expressed his 'sentiments of commiseration [for] the very wretched state of the Aborigines of this Country'. Because he wanted to ameliorate 'their condition…and improve the energies of this innocent and unoffending Race', he announced that he would embark on 'an experiment so interesting to the feelings of Humanity'. He conceded that the colonial project had excluded 'Indigenous people from 'many of the natural advantages they have previously derived from the animal and other productions of this part of the territory', praised the fact that they had displayed 'a disposition to submit peaceably to such establishments as were necessarily made on the part of the British Government on the formation of this settlement', and said that he wanted to 'effect the Civilization of the Aborigines of New South Wales and to render their habits more domesticated and industrious'.

Macquarie was excited by this project, which he regarded as a fresh and ingenious approach to improving race relations. Instead of describing Indigenous people ('Aborigines') as savage, primitive and barbarous as was usually the case, here Macquarie portrayed them as victims who, like hapless objects, would be subjected to an 'interesting' experiment. He also described them as 'innocent and unoffending', that is, as childlike creatures who needed to be cultivated and taught so that they would become 'domesticated and industrious'. In similar vein, Macquarie alluded to the primitive, 'undeveloped' nature of the Indigenous people by referring to the fact that they were sustained by 'animal and other productions', that is, not by manufactured products, as enjoyed by developed people.

It appears that Macquarie was the first governor to use the term 'aborigine' instead of 'native'. Knapman noted that, in the discourse of colonial administrators and theorisers, the term 'aborigine' was becoming more prevalent during the early nineteenth century:

> The transition from using the terms 'savage' and 'barbarian' to 'abo-

riginal' or 'indigenous' was not a mere replacement of words. Instead, it introduced the idea of 'aboriginal' peoples as a distinct ethnic identity associated with social form. The aboriginal condition became a focus of study.

The term was also useful to distinguish the Australian-born generation that was emerging in settler society. For instance, in a letter dated 8 March 1817, colonial-born Elizabeth Macarthur, the daughter of John and Elizabeth Macarthur, referred to herself as a 'native' who was writing about 'native' matters. 'Native' derives from the Latin word for 'birth', and thus Australian-born settlers were also 'natives', whereas 'aboriginal' denoted those whose ancestry in the country dated from the earliest times and had no other, discoverable place of ancestry.

The *Sydney Gazette* of 31 December 1814 reported the next development in Macquarie's civilising project. Accompanied by senior officials, at Parramatta he met with less than sixty Indigenous people 'of all ages and sexes'. The governor 'conversed with them for an hour, pointing out in an affable and familiar way the advantages they would necessarily derive from a change of manners, and an application to moderate industry'. After 'three children were yielded up to the benevolent purposes of the Institution', roast beef and ale were served.

The newspaper attributed the poor turnout to misunderstanding, namely, 'the more distant tribes…suspiciously [imagined] that they were to be forcibly deprived of their children, and themselves sent to labour'. One wonders what pressures were exerted to get Indigenous parents to 'yield up' their children. Did suspicions about the governor's designs on children exacerbate the frontier conflict?

On 1 March 1815, the *Gazette* reported that there were thirteen pupils at the Native Institution, where they were making excellent progress 'not commonly excelled by children of any colour or complexion whatsoever'. Furthermore, the children so much appreciated their 'improved condition' that they did not want to leave the school. On 24 March 1815, Macquarie wrote to the Colonial Secretary, Lord Bathurst, that the number of children had fallen to six because some parents, 'from an unaccountable Caprice have since decoyed away their Children'. However, he was confident that the institution would be a success when the 'Elder Natives' saw how much the pupils improved in health, cleanliness and personal appearance, and abandoned their suspicions about European intentions. In fact, Macquarie was confident that 'their Repugnance to Civilization will soon yield and be entirely Overcome'.

Macquarie also told Lord Bathurst that he had settled sixteen families on land on the north shore of the harbour. They had been provided with tools and implements, as well as a boat, and he was sure that 'they will become Industrious, and set a good Example to the other Native Tribes residing in the Vicinity of Port Jackson'.

On 4 December 1815, Lord Bathurst wrote that he was pleased that Macquarie 'had reason to entertain a more favorable opinion of the General Character and Habits of the Natives of New Holland, who were resident in the Vicinity of the Colony, than that which has been hitherto generally promulgated'. In fact, there was so much interest in the natives that any project that tended to advance their appreciation of the 'Benefits of Civilisation' was sure to meet with the approval of the Prince Regent. Also, Lord Bathurst was pleased to note that the project was well within budget. That being the case, 'no Objection whatever can exist to immediately adopting the plan which you have suggested for carrying it into effect'.

We don't know what most colonists thought about the Native Institution, if they thought about it at all. However, at least one settler approved of it; in a letter dated 8 March 1817, young Elizabeth Macarthur termed it the outcome of 'the benevolent exertions of Governor Macquarie' and hoped that 'in the hands of Providence' the products of the school 'may be instrumental in civilizing their countrymen'.

With the tacit approval of royalty and the consent of the colonial secretary, the civilising project was under way. However, there was a big fly in the ointment, namely the rising violence on the southern frontier of the colony. Although we do not have records of the settlers' attitudes and opinions, it is certain that they wanted action, and wanted it soon.

They would not have been prepared to wait until the civilising project began to have its beneficial effects on the natives' attitudes and actions – whenever and however that might happen.

On 10 April 1816, Macquarie acted by sending out three military detachments. Now, with the gloves of reconciliation and understanding removed, the *Sydney Gazette* of 13 April 1816 reported that the soldiers had been mobilised 'for the protection of the out settlements against the violent and flagitious conduct of the hostile natives'.

Four days later, on 17 April, the 'Appin Massacre' occurred, when one of the detachments attacked a camp at night and killed about fourteen Indigenous men, women and children. (The actual number is uncertain.) Most of them died in flight, by falling to their death over a cliff and into a ravine. The soldiers strung up the bodies of two warriors in trees and took captive two women and three children. (Again, the number is disputed.)

However, the incident did not end the confrontations. Less than a month later, on 4 May 1816, an exasperated Macquarie issued a proclamation that began with the words

> Whereas the ABORIGINES, or Black NATIVES of this Colony, have for the last three Years manifested a strong and sanguinary Spirit of ANIMOSITY and HOSTILITY towards the BRITISH INHABITANTS residing in the Interior and remote Parts of the Territory, and been recently guilty of most atrocious and wanton Barbarities, in indiscriminately murdering Men, Women, and Children from whom they had received no Offence or Provocation; and also in killing the Cattle, and plundering and destroying the Grain and Property of every Description…

He continued by saying that the authorities had 'acted with the utmost Lenity and Humanity' in the hope that it would 'conciliate them to the British Government'. However, this having failed, the governor had sent out a military force because it was 'reluctantly compelled to resort to coercive and strong Measures to prevent the Recurrence of such Crimes and Barbarities'. He regretted that 'some few innocent

Men, Women, and Children' had been killed along with 'some of the most guilty and atrocious of the Natives', and hoped that this would end the attacks on people and property.

Macquarie then ordered that no Indigenous person was to appear within a mile of any settlement 'armed with any warlike or offensive Weapon or Weapons of any Description'; that any group of Indigenous people near a settlement should not number more than six persons; that ceremonial gatherings at which fighting took place were banned; and that natives who wished to be considered under the protection of the British government should apply for passports or certificates to that effect.

In the proclamation, the governor 'earnestly exhorts, and thus publicly invites the Natives to relinquish their wandering, idle, and predatory Habits of Life, and to become industrious and useful Members of a Community'. To that end, he was willing to grant plots of land, together with implements and provisions, to any Indigenous persons who wanted to become farmers. He also encouraged them to find employment as labourers. Finally, he announced 'a general Friendly Meeting of all the Natives residing in the Colony' on 28 December at Parramatta, at which he would explain the purpose of the institution for children and consult 'with them on the best Means of improving their present Condition'.

On 11 May, the *Sydney Gazette* carried a report of the military campaign and described the events at Appin as follows:

> It appears that the party under Capt. Wallis, fell in with a number of the natives on the 17th ult. near Mr. Broughton's farm, in the Airds District, and killed fourteen of them, taking two women and three children prisoners. Amongst the killed were found the bodies of two of the most hostile of the natives, called Durelle and Conibigal.

The writer praised 'the humanity with which this necessary but unpleasant duty has been conducted throughout' and stated that although not as successful as hoped for, it would prevent 'a recurrence of those barbarities which the natives have of late so frequently committed on the unprotected Settlers and their Families'.

Attacks continued in the vicinity of Kurrajong, which is in the foothills of the Blue Mountains near Windsor. On 13 July 1816, the *Gazette* reported,

> Another murder was perpetrated by the natives… The victim to their barbarity was Joseph Hobson, who is stated to have been the only settler remaining on that line of farms, in consequence of the excesses lately committed… The miscreants afterwards clove the head of the unfortunate sufferer, and brutally mangled the body.

Macquarie responded with a proclamation dated 20 July 1816, in which he expressed his regret that some 'hostile Natives' had ignored the offer to come under the protection of the government while continuing to 'commit several further atrocious Acts of Barbarity on the unoffending and unprotected Settlers and their Families'. He outlawed ten individuals by name and put a price of ten pounds on each of their heads. He also ordered the magistrates in the Hawkesbury and Nepean districts to organise settler self-defence groups and announced how and where military detachments would be stationed.

On 31 August 1816, the *Gazette* carried a grim report about frontier violence. In the Newcastle area, six absconded convicts had been killed by Indigenous people, while at Mulgoa on the Nepean River, a shepherd had been killed and his flock of about two hundred sheep had been destroyed. Based on information received, the report warned,

> It may evidently be implied that a connexion or correspondence must subsist between the hordes in our vicinity, and those considerably to the northward, and that all within this circle of communication are determined upon the destruction of every white person that may unhappily fall into their power.

Furthermore, the report stated that 'they [Indigenous people] no longer act in small predatory parties, as heretofore, but now carry the appearance of an extensive combination…'

Information is patchy, but the Appin Massacre, although a standout atrocity, was only one among many bloody encounters at the time. Also, months after the event, there was still significant resistance in various parts of the colonial frontier, to the extent that, as seen, settlers even had to abandon one forward position on the frontier.

On 4 April 1817, in a dispatch to Earl Bathurst, Macquarie reported that on 28 December 1816, a general meeting with Indigenous people was held at Parramatta,

> when I gave them a plentiful Treat of Meat and Drink; on which occasion 179 Men, Women and Children were assembled, being a greater Number than had been seen together at any one time for Several Years past...

Everyone attending the meeting seemed to be 'happy and perfectly Satisfied', and some of the Indigenous attenders freely 'gave up' their children to attend the Native Institution. Macquarie expressed the hope that the progress that had already been made at the institution 'will ultimately pave the way for the Civilization of a large Portion of the Aborigines of the Country'. The civilising mission was back on track.

What happened at the annual general meetings with Indigenous people, apart from the consumption of generous amounts of food and drink? Macquarie's notification of the event for 1817 informed readers that at the meeting, 'His Excellency the Governor will confer and advise with them [Indigenous people] on the Plan of Life they may be inclined to adopt for their own Comfort and Happiness...' Clearly, Macquarie remained resolute in his aim to transform the culture and orientation of Indigenous people so that they would become domesticated within colonial society. It was an ambitious aim.

In his dispatch of 4 April 1817, Macquarie also told Earl Bathurst that he had been compelled to introduce measures for 'Quelling and Subduing the hostile Spirit of Violence and Rapine, which the black Natives or Aborigines of this Country had for a Considerable time past Manifested against the White Inhabitants...' The measures had been so successful that 'all Hostility on both Sides has long since Ceased; the black Natives living now peaceably and quietly in every part of the Colony, Unmolested by the White Inhabitants'.

For the moment, the colony was free of Indigenous armed resistance, both within and without its borders. But this was only a temporary situation; more land theft would be met by more resistance. In the same dispatch, Macquarie noted 'how very much this Colony has lately been Extended in Consequence of the recent Discoveries to the Westward of the Blue Mountains, and to the Southward as far as Shoal Haven', and requested that the military force should be increased by 'two regiments, comprising one thousand two hundred men, to guard against any Internal Insurrection or Commotion, or a Recurrence of Hostilities on the part of the Native Blacks…'

To return to 1816: what happened to the Indigenous communities who had been involved in the resistance? Although we don't know how many Indigenous people lived on and near the western and southern frontiers, they must have been quite numerous. For instance, as seen, on 7 May 1814, the *Sydney Gazette* reported an attack by 400 warriors. These would have been men and older boys of 'military' age, representing perhaps thirty per cent of their base communities, at most. That implies a total number of about 1,300 persons. However, it is likely that a greater number of Indigenous people would have inhabited the whole 'resistance' region, which stretched from the mountains, across the Nepean area, to the adjacent coast. What happened to these people, perhaps a few thousand in number, when resistance ended? Some might have been absorbed into the colony, as labourers. However, there was plenty of convict labour available, so there would not have been much need for Indigenous servants.

Some might have taken up grants of land, and some might have gone to the 'reserves' that Macquarie created within the colonial borders. However, the numbers involved in these options would have been small.

Some might have fallen back onto country that traditionally belonged to other groups, where they would have been 'absorbed', whether peacefully or otherwise. There is a suggestion of this in Strachan's biography of missionary Samuel Leigh, where the author wrote about Indigenous people that, 'Being terror-struck, and finding themselves unable to cope with civilized man, they fell back into the depths of their native forests.' However, this was written a long time after the events, and not by someone who was close to the locality, so it might not be trustworthy.

Some might have died because of disease and privation.

It is likely that many more Indigenous people died from violence and associated causes than was reported. For instance, Strachan reported that Leigh wrote during August 1817,

> About nine months since, we were much disturbed by the natives who speared a number of stockmen and others in the interior of the country. The governor sent out several detachments of soldiers, who drove them from the settlements, and shot many of them in the woods.

How many would 'many of them' have been?

We don't have the answers. But what of it? For the settlers, what mattered was, as Macquarie wrote, that 'all Hostility on both Sides has long since Ceased; the black Natives living now peaceably and quietly in every part of the Colony…' Now that the issue was out of the way, the colonists could get on with the important things in life, undisturbed – getting and spending, ploughing and harvesting, acquiring land and wealth, and all the rest of the activities that contribute to happy and successful lives in a country of golden soil and boundless plains.

Twelve
Conclusion

In this book, I have traced settler perspectives on Indigenous Australians during the early years of colonisation from 1788 until 1816. I noted that because the book enters a busy field that is covered by accomplished writers and scholars, I have to offer something different and worthwhile. I hope that I have done so.

To sum up, I will begin by narrating an experience that I had when I was a young man of about thirty years of age in South Africa which, as I said, was the country of my birth, and the place where I grew up and spent the early years of my adult life. In those days, under the apartheid-era Group Areas Act, people of various 'races' were forced to live in segregated residential areas. Invariably, white people got the best slice of cake because the White group areas always included the business and commercial centers, together with the inner suburbs. Many white people got good deals by buying property from people of other 'races' who had been 'endorsed out' and had to sell up.

During the mid-1970s, I lived in a small town where the business area and adjacent parts had been proclaimed a 'White area'. Close to where I lived, there was a house that was occupied by 'Coloured' people. The family had owned and occupied the properties for several generations, until they were forced to sell when the Group Areas Act was implemented. Because of the small size of the town, there was no 'Coloured residential area', so they lived in a 'White area'. However, they could not own property in a 'White area'. Consequently, they remained in the house that they had formerly owned, but where they now lived as tenants of the white man who had bought the properties. In fact, their landlord owned a builders' supply company – only white people could own businesses within the town area – and some of the family members worked for him.

The man who told me this story was one of the tenants. It was a tale of injustice, humiliation and greed, in which he and his family had come off badly. Understandably, he was frustrated and angry.

I remembered the story when I wrote about Bennelong leading his people into the colonial settlement, which was located on land that they had once owned and had called home since time immemorial. Now they were like tenants, who were only allowed there at the pleasure of the new owners, the settlers, who dictated all the terms of occupancy and use.

At least Bennelong and his fellows got a relatively good 'deal'. The same could not be said for other groups, as the frontier expanded, absorbing more and more land, and as more and more Indigenous people were affected. Whether they opposed the tide of colonisation or gave in without much resistance, the result was the same: the survivors became 'tenants' on land that they had once owned. There they lived as labourers or odd jobbers, among other modes of existence, while a few inhabited 'reserves' that had been allocated to them.

I was struck by the fact that amid the many dispatches, journals, reports, articles and books that I read while preparing this book, there were few places where writers acknowledged that land theft and dispossession were central to the poor relationship between settlers and Indigenous people. Although Phillip did so on several occasions, having done so, he almost immediately shied away and identified other reasons for Indigenous hostility, as if he was surprised and embarrassed by what he had admitted. There were a few other admissions, always from authority figures, of which the most forthright was the statement by Governor King, who wrote of Indigenous people, 'I have ever considered them the real Proprietors of the Soil…'

For the rest, there was silence on the issue. For authority figures, admitting the truth exposed their predicament. On the one hand, they were instructed 'to extend your intercourse with the natives and to conciliate their affections, enjoining all our subjects to live in amity and kindness with them...' However, the governors' main task was to preside over the well-being and growth of the colony. The two tasks were incompatible. Something had to give, and it was never going to be the well-being and growth of the colony.

There is no evidence that 'ordinary' colonists admitted that Indigenous people were angry and hostile because of land theft and dispossession. Among the reasons for this would be that most accepted the imperial narrative that Europeans were entitled to territory that was occupied by non-Europeans; secondly, that to survive, the early 'settlers', namely convicts and military personnel, had no choice but to overcome the new and strange conditions with which they were faced – including the hostility of Indigenous people; and thirdly, that the only authority that settlers recognised, namely the state and its representative, the governor, had legitimately granted them the land.

Settler perceptions of Indigenous people grew harsher and less nuanced during the years between 1788 and 1816. Although, like almost all other Europeans, the officer-commentators thought that Indigenous people were 'savages' who lived primitive lives in inexplicable discomfort, they did have a lively and thorough interest in many aspects of Indigenous lives, customs and conventions. In addition, they saw some Indigenous people as individuals and 'humanised' them by portraying their personalities, habits, characteristics and mannerisms.

One might have thought that there would have been greater understanding and mutual sympathy when rapprochement took place and Indigenous people freely entered, lived in and exited the settlement. After all, soon after rapprochement began, Tench wrote, 'our greatest source of entertainment now lay in cultivating the acquaintance of our new friends, the natives'. However, this did not happen. Instead, although the two races interacted, often sharing interconnected spaces, they largely kept apart in discrete social spheres. (The existence of the Sydney Pidgin testifies to social distance.) In time, they moved further apart. Even Bennelong, who was by far the most likely Indigenous person to integrate with European customs and culture, turned back to traditional life. As an article in the *Sydney Gazette* of 28 July 1810 noted, 'Formerly our intercourse with the natives was much greater than at present…but that intimacy has subsided.'

However, rapprochement was only a small, somewhat bright blip on the foggy radar of relations between the races. Confrontation and conflict mounted as the frontier moved outwards and onwards, gobbling up Indigenous land. At the same time, as always happens when there is fierce conflict, European attitudes hardened and soon even the governors, who were instructed to 'extend your Intercourse with the Natives, and to conciliate their Affections', freely used terms such as 'barbaric', 'unenlightened', 'violent' and 'wanton'. Mrs John Macarthur's opinion, expressed during 1816, probably represented the views of many settlers when she wrote, 'Attempts have been made to civilise the natives of this country, but they are complete savages, and are as lawless and troublesome as when the Colony was first established.'

There was one exception to the dismal, downward-trending perspective that settlers had on Indigenous people. That was Governor Macquarie's 'civilising mission', where he proposed that Indigenous people could become 'industrious and useful Members of a Community'. Although his condescending approach was still predicated on the proposition that Indigenous people were savage and barbarous, with the added caveat that experience had shown that the adults were incapable of becoming 'civilised,' he did at least suggest a way forward for the relationship. However, his was a top-down view that was not shared by most of the population.

The great and seemingly growing gap between the two races might have been presaged by the 'inadequacies' in the early descriptions of Indigenous life, manners and customs. I noted that despite all that was written about Indigenous people during the early years, there was one issue that was hardly addressed, namely the 'world view' of Indigenous people, including law, diffuse responsibility roles, the relationship of a clan to a wider body, ideas of justice, and Dreaming, with its connection to the cosmos of the past. I concluded that when describing Indigenous people, the early commentators were like a man laboriously peeling an onion, but only up to a certain point: although he removed many layers, he did not get anywhere near the core.

If the early settlers had attempted to attain deeper understanding, might they have had less antagonistic perspectives on Indigenous people during the decades that followed? Probably not. The main issue was always land theft and dispossession, and no amount of 'understanding' would ever have got past that, especially as land theft, which deprived Indigenous people of 'the means of procuring their daily subsistence' (Eyre, 1845), also involved forcing a severance of the intense attachment and care that Indigenous people had for 'country', as well as violating sacred places, with their association with Dreaming.

After the early, small blip of rapprochement had passed from the radar screen, the developing settler perspective was that Indigenous people were no more than annoying, unappealing obstacles to colonial expansion and land possession. When they were eliminated as obstacles, it was best if the survivors (however many, or however few) were domesticated and sidelined.

As I said earlier, in 1845 John Eyre wrote that although Indigenous people had once evinced 'the fearless courage and proud demeanor which a life of independence and freedom always inspires', only fifty-seven years after European settlement began, they were 'strangers in their own land and possess no longer the usual means of procuring their daily subsistence; hungry, and famished, they wander about begging...'

As T.S. Eliot wrote, 'In my beginning is my end.'

Works cited

Bradley, William. About 1802. *A voyage to New South Wales*. Manuscript digitised photocopy A3631. State Library of New South Wales

Blackburn, David. Undated. Letters received by Richard Knight, 12 July 1788, 19 March 1791. State Library of New South Wales

Bladen, F. M., Alexander Britton, and James Cook. (1892). Historical records of New South Wales. Retrieved August 26, 2019, from http://nla.gov.au/nla.obj-359771272

Burke, Edmund. 1790. *Reflections on the Revolution in France, and on the proceedings in certain societies in London relative to that event. In a letter intended to have been sent to a gentleman in Paris*, first edition. London: J.Dodsley in Pall Mall

Collins, David. 1798. *An account of the English colony of NSW*. London

Eyre, John. 1845. *Journals of expeditions of discovery into central Australia and overland from Adelaide to King George's Sound in the years 1840–1: Volume 1*. London: T. and W. Boone

Gewald, Jan-Bart. 1996. *Towards Redemption: A Socio-Political History of the Herero of Namibia between 1890 and 1923*. Leiden: Research School CNWS, School of Asian, African, and Amerindian Studies

Holt, Joseph. 1838. *Memoirs of Joseph Holt, general of the Irish rebels in 1798*. London: Henry Colburn, Publisher

Hunter, John. 1793. *An historical journal of the transactions at Port Jackson and Norfolk Island, with the discoveries that have been made in New South Wales and the Southern Ocean since the publication of Phillip's voyage*. London: John Stockdale

King, Robert J. 1986. 'Eora and the English at Port Jackson: a Spanish view', *Aboriginal History*, 10.1

Knapman, Gareth. 2017. *Race and British colonialism in South-East Asia, 1770–1870: John Crawfurd and the politics of equality*. New York and London: Routledge

Knapman, Gareth and Martin Müller. 2019. 'Protector of Aborigines or war criminal: two opposing liberal views of James Brooke.' In Gareth Knapman, Anthony Milner and Mary Quilty, eds. *Liberalism and the British Empire in Southeast Asia*. New York: Routledge

Lichtenstein, Hinrich. 1815. *Travels in Southern Africa in the years 1803, 1804, 1805 and 1806* (translated by Anne Plumtree), London: Henry Colburn

Macquarie, Lachlan. Memoranda & Related Papers. 22 December 1808-14 July 1823. Original held in the Mitchell Library, Sydney.ML Ref: A772 29f. [Microfilm Reel CY301 Frame #36].

Mann, D.D. 1811. *The present picture of New South Wales*. London: John Booth

Marsden, J.B. 1913. *Life and Work of Samuel Marsden*. Christchurch, Wellington and Dunedin, NZ; Melbourne and London: Whitcombe & Tombs Limited

Massie, R.H. 1905. *The native tribes of the Transvaal*. Great Britain: War Office.

Moodie, J.W.D. 1835. *Ten years in South Africa*. London: Richard Bentley

Morgan, John. 1852. *The life and adventures of William Buckley thirty-two years a wanderer amongst the aborigines of then unexplored country around Port Phillip, now the province of Victoria*. Hobart: A. Macdougall

Peron, M.F. 1809. *A voyage of discovery to the Southern Hemisphere* (translated from the French). London: Richard Phillips

Petrie, Constance Campbell. 1904. *Tom Petrie's reminiscences of early Queensland*. Brisbane: Watson, Ferguson

Phillip, Arthur. 1789. *The voyage of Governor Phillip to Botany Bay*. London: John Stockdale

Powell, Michael and Rex Hesline. 2010. 'Making tribes? Constructing Aboriginal tribal entities in Sydney and coastal NSW from the early colonial period to the present', *Journal of the Royal Australian Historical Society*. 96.2

Roe, Michael. 1958. 'Philip Gidley King'. *The Australian Quarterly*, 30.3

Smith, Keith Vincent. 2009. 'Bennelong among his people', *Aboriginal History*, vol. 3

Strachan, Alexander. 1873. *Remarkable incidents in the life of the Rev. Samuel Leigh*. London: Hamilton, Adams and Co.

Steinmetz, George. 2005. 'The First Genocide of the 20th Century and its Postcolonial Afterlives: Germany and the Namibian Ovaherero', *The Journal of the International Institute*, 12.2

Tench, Watkin. 1789. *A narrative of the expedition to Botany Bay*. London: J. Debrett

—. 1793. *A complete account of the settlement at Port Jackson*. London: G. Nicol and J. Sewell

Thompson, George. 1827. *Travels and adventures in Southern Africa*. London: Henry Colburn

—. *Journal.* In Early News from a New Colony: British Museum Papers. (updated 2013, accessed 31 July 2019)

Tuckey, James Hingston. 1805. *An Account of the Voyage to establish a Colony at Port Phillip.* London: Longman Hurst Rees & Orme

Turner, Frederick Jackson. 1921. *The frontier in American history.* New York: Henry Holt and Company

Watling, Thomas. 1794. (PDF). Penrith, Scotland: Ann Bell

White, Maggie. 2011. Pathways to a good life well lived. Report by Herculeia Consulting, Perth

www.ingramcontent.com/pod-product-compliance
Lightning Source LLC
Chambersburg PA
CBHW030905080526
44589CB00010B/158